POWER AND PERSUASION

POWER AND PERSUASION

How to Command Success In Business and Your Personal Life

MICHAEL MASTERSON

WILEY

John Wiley & Sons, Inc.

Published by John Wiley & Sons, Inc., Hoboken, New Jersey
Published simultaneously in Canada

For general information on our other products and services or for technical support, please contact our Customer Care Department within the United States at (800) 762-2974, outside the United States at (317) 572-3993 or fax (317) 572-4002.

Wiley also publishes its books in a variety of electronic formats. Some content that appears in print may not be available in electronic books. For more information about Wiley products, visit our web site at www.wiley.com.

ISBN-13: 978-0-471-7-86771
ISBN-10: 0-471786-772

Printed in the United States of America

10 9 8 7 6 5 4 3 2 1

CONTENTS

DEDICATION

To Lilian Feder, who let me retake my Greek mythology
test if I promised to dedicate a book to her.

ACKNOWLEDGMENTS

Susan Clark for pulling together all my relevant writings on the subject, assembling them in a rational flow and writing many of the transitional paragraphs; Judy Strauss and Susan Horrowitz for editing out so many of my faults; Charlie Byrne and Jessica Haynes for their thoughtful comments; Will Bonner and Maggie Crowell for directing all the confusion; Lisa Bruette and Patrick Coffey for the marketing; Kathy Osborne for her design; Mike Ward, Wayne Ellis, and MaryBeth Wheless for their insight; Debra Englander at John Wiley for her published sense and Kathryn Fitzgerald for teaching me how to follow.

INTRODUCTION

"A leader is a dealer in hope."
~Napoleon Bonaparte, *Military Maxims*, 1804–15

Throw three darts at the Table of Contents of any business magazine or newsletter and chances are very good that you have barbed an article on leadership.

Leadership is today's tipping point business idea. It has replaced excellence as the go-to concept in seminars and boardrooms. Figuring out what good leadership is and how to make it happen are favorite topics among business schoolteachers, corporate executives, and management consultants.

Like most popular concepts, some half-baked notions and even a few potentially false ideas have become popular today. For example:

- The first job of a business leader should be to make his employees happy.
- Effective leaders are patient, kind, considerate and fair minded.
- To lead well you must be inclusive and collaborative.

- Team building is the essence of good leadership.
- Diversity and fairness are hallmarks of the superior leader.

I'm not saying that goodness, kindness and fair play aren't admirable qualities in a leader. But when I think about my experience in business—what I actually did, rather than what I'd like to have done—I see that much of this sort of politically correct behavior was conspicuously absent.

And it's not just me. Of the many successful leaders I've worked with and have talked about in *Early To Rise* (my daily e-zine, earlytorise.com) most were a complicated mix of powerful, positive qualities and some negative ones. For example:

- LW: Extremely pushy, fun-loving megalomaniac.
- JSN: Intimidating. Fear provoking. A stickler for details.
- GP: Paranoid. Secretive. Kind.
- SK: Never had an original idea in his head. Worried about employees who did.
- BB: Refuses to give direction. Can't negotiate.

If you want to be a successful leader—and I can't think of any area of activity that this would not apply to—you have to deal with groups of people. Whether your goal is to conduct an orchestra, direct a martial arts expert, or be the head of a hundred million dollar business; getting your objectives accomplished will require the cooperation of dozens and more likely hundreds (or even thousands) of people along the way.

A leader's primary job is to get people to do what needs to be done. There are fundamentally two ways of doing that. The first and most common approach is to bully people into following. The leader that bribes, demeans, threatens and shouts can get work done. But there are costs in using force. And the primary cost is the loss of loyalty. The leader who bullies his way through can be effective so long as he holds power, but the moment power slips away, so does his effectiveness. If his power weakens sufficiently everyone who can will turn against him.

The other way to get people to do what needs to be done is to inspire them. Inspiration means to fill with spirit or animation. A leader who persuades others to follow him, not by force, but rather by inspiration creates a bank of good will that stays with him, even if and when his personal power disappears.

If getting people to do the work is the first job of a leader, creating and promoting a view of what that work will look like, once completed is a close second. Successful leaders need not be clever or original, but they must have a good and attractive idea about the future of their business.

Sometimes these visions are clear; other times they are nebulous. Sometimes they are logical; other times they're inconsistent. Some leaders think in terms of dollars, others, in terms of products. Still others have visions that involve size, scope, or even geography.

One of the best and most successful business leaders I know always imagines his company as an internationalized "beehive" of smart ideas. He doesn't define it that way. In fact, he never defines it at all. But when he talks about what new products "make sense" for the business and why "it might be a good idea" to open up a new office in Cape Town, his employees get the picture, however impressionistic.

He never sends out memos outlining his vision. But he writes thoughtful essays on why one product or service is more valuable than another. He dislikes talking about financial goals and resists conversations about company morale. His answer to individual complaints is to ignore them. When key executives present him with problems, he shrugs his shoulders and tells them, "Gee, I don't know what you should do."

He's not interested in organizational charts, almost never reads financial statements, and has a healthy revulsion to terms like "human capital," "team building," and "collaboration." In hiring people, he cares nothing about experience, credentials, or compatibility. He considers only two things, intelligence and character.

He is uncomfortable with conflict, avoids disputes of any kind (even if it may cost him money) and is generally considered a pushover when negotiating. He doesn't like giving raises—even to his best people—but he is happy to pay top dollar for talent that requests it.

He believes in firing weak people, but has never done so himself.

He likes hiring strong people, but then leaves them without any idea of what the job entails or how to do it.

In short, he breaks most of the rules for good leadership except that he has a compelling vision about the future and a capacity to persuade.

These two traits have created and grown a large, interesting, profitable, thriving company that sells good ideas to millions of people around the world.

So if you read nothing else about leadership, know this: that if you can learn the art of persuasion and lock on to a compelling vision you have all you really need to be a great leader.

That said, there is much more to great leadership than these two essentials. In the following pages I've tried to distinguish what I think is essential in good leadership from what is merely desirable. I've made many recommendations, for example, that I lack the discipline to follow. Still, nothing you'll read here is theoretical. My experience bore each of these ideas, and some of them, I hope, will help you.

PART ONE

SO YOU WANT TO BE A LEADER?

[KEY POINT]

It's difficult to learn leadership skills and strategies. One reason is that the popular press perpetuates myths based on distorted and sometimes inaccurate second-hand information. Some of the most damaging myths promote "soft" leadership skills, employee participation in the wrong areas, ineffective teamwork, employee empowerment and a system of employee rewards. But the truth is, great leaders focus only one thing: creating and communicating a compelling, inspiring vision. They spend time thinking about how to make things better in the workplace. They discover how to make the Work worthwhile, then distill it down to a phrase or philosophy that can easily be communicated to their employees.

CHAPTER 1:
WHAT YOU NEED (AND DON'T) TO BE A GOOD LEADER

"Don't confuse getting in front with getting out front. That's the difference between a principal and a spokesman, between a mover and a shaker."

~William Safire, *Leadership:*
A Treasury of Great Quotations for Those Who Aspire to Lead[1]

Did you know that the average age of the people who write for *Forbes, Fortune, Business Week* and the *Wall Street Journal* is something like 29 years old? Take a look at the masthead of almost any business magazine and what do you see? The names of—more likely

---

1 Safir, Leonard, Safire, William, *Leadership: A Treasury of Great Quotations for Those Who Aspire to Lead* (Galahad Books, September 2000).

than not—young women.

If you read the likes of *Harvard Business Review* and other "prestigious" publications you'll be reading theories propounded by college professors and research analysts.

Don't get me wrong. I read these publications. And I understand the necessity of hiring young, inexperienced writers. But because I have been on the inside of the business publishing world I've become skeptical about what I read in the business press, and especially so about advice that is given.

Such is the case with the business advice I read about leadership. For the most part, the ideas seem wrong to me. They don't correspond to anything I've experienced myself and they don't equate with business practices I've seen as a consultant to business owners. It's not a conspiracy. It's the process that's the problem. I know how second-hand information works. It gets misunderstood, oversimplified and distorted. And if that's not bad enough it also gets cleaned up, edited, prettified. Not, in the latter case, by the writers, but by the experts who are being interviewed. (When asked about the secret to his success, what business leader wouldn't want to give motivating credit to his troops?)

Good business writers know how to recognize an interesting idea and present it in a clear, convincing manner. That is good—so long as the idea itself is good. But if the idea is wrong . . . then the good writing only serves to waste your time or harm you. And there are a lot of bad ideas out there right now. In fact, I believe there are 10 prevalent myths about leadership in circulation, all of which can do damage to your business if you follow them. Let's see how they are wrong and what techniques the REAL leaders use.

MYTH #1: "SOFT" LEADERSHIP SKILLS WORK

I read an article recently in which a spokesman for Office Team, a business consulting firm, said that "if companies want to be successful in the future they'll have to adopt soft leadership skills." By this he meant listening to employees, sharing feelings with them, and keeping an open mind "to all kinds of ideas—even bad ones."

If you don't learn these soft skills, the consultancy says, then you will soon be in trouble as these softer skills "completely replace the older, harder skills of planning, persuasion, and discipline." OfficeTeam says: "The future office environment won't allow for command-and-control focused management style. Employees want to contribute to decisions and offer creative solutions." This sort of thinking completely contradicts my own experience. From what I've seen, most employees want leadership. And leadership to them means that someone else solves the problems and tells them what to do about them.

GOOD LEADERS INSPIRE WORK

As a leader in your business, you are earning big bucks to do the hard thinking, to make the tough decisions, and to get the job done, even if it means pushing the weight up hill. Yes, you should be open to new ideas. Yes, you should talk to the rank-and-file workers. Yes, you should pay attention to your employees. But the big decisions about where to go and what to make and how to solve your problems are ultimately yours to solve.

This requires vision, knowledge, skill and most certainly, good ideas. But even more important is the understanding of how to get people to embrace your ideas and to work to achieve them, even in the face of criticism and adversity.

So how do you do it? By making the work seem worthwhile. For a perfect example look to the great religious leaders of history, from Jesus Christ to Gandhi, these leaders were able to persuade large groups of people to do all kinds of great and difficult work merely by creating the idea that the work itself was good. (Yes, there may have been some bribing going on there—the promise of heaven and all that, but I can't imagine so many people could have made so many small yet difficult daily sacrifices without believing that the work itself was worthwhile.)

MYTH #2 "ALLOWING PARTICIPATION IS MORE IMPORTANT THAN SHARING YOUR VISION."

Yet another gem from an article gleamed in a prestigious business publication. The essays said that when it comes to setting goals, leaders should focus on fostering and improving employee participation above creating a plan for better business.

That is just silly, utterly silly. It's so silly; in fact that I wondered if I was reading an old, April 1 issue. No I wasn't. This was a serious recommendation offered up in sober language by some no-doubt earnest young writer quoting from some ex-tough-guy business person who wanted to sugar coat his career.

Back to reality—a leader *can* delegate a great deal of responsibility if he surrounds himself with good people, but the one thing he can never delegate is the job of establishing goals and creating a vision— that is unless he wants to cease being a leader.

Dreaming about what your business can accomplish, thinking about how far it can go and how great it can be is the *most important* job you can do. If you are a leader, you must spend much of your spare time doing that.

Yes, you can ask questions. Yes, you can seek advice. But when it comes down to deciding where you want to go and what you want to achieve, you've got to do it yourself. Then you've got to share your vision.

GOOD LEADERS COMMUNICATE A COMPELLING VISION

It is not easy to inspire work. Those that can do so have one thing in common. They have a keen ability to create and communicate a compelling vision. This is essential for effective leadership. Most real authorities on leadership recognize this. You can be fairly limited in other intellectual qualities—but strong in audacity and the ability to communicate a picture—and still be a successful leader. (Ronald Reagan proved that, didn't he?)

The same can be said for leaders of social causes. When ordinary citizens work tirelessly to respond to a crisis or natural disaster, they do so not for any of the normal reasons employees work; but because they feel they are compelled by a vision. They feel engaged in a worthwhile process.

Think about religion today. All those apostles you see at airports.

Why do they work like that? Why do they submit themselves to that kind of indignity? It's not for the money. They get none. And it's not for public approval; they get the opposite. They shave their heads, put on the robes of their religion and spend countless hours begging because they believe that what they are doing is good. It's as simple— and as powerful—as that.

To be a great leader you have to spend time thinking about how you can make things better and then make people believe in the goodness of your ideas.

If you can do that they will work for you. They will beg for you. They will fight for you. And—in extreme cases (not that this is something you'd hope for)—they may even die for you.

MYTH #3 EMPLOYEE HAPPINESS IS KEY.

The newly appointed publisher of the *Wall Street Journal*, Karen Elliott House, is working hard to make the paper's employees "feel happy and appreciated," according to an article in a recent issue of The *New York Times*. When employees are happy, "that's when everyone works best," she says. This is a common view among workers and new managers, but it's not one held by me. In fact it's not one held by many of the experienced managers I know.

Effective managers don't spend their time trying to make people feel appreciated. Why? Because it doesn't work. And because it doesn't help.

And mostly because that's not what they are paid to do. They are paid to make the business grow by producing and selling good products and services. This is an outward-looking goal. It is about the customers and the value that is given to them. Worrying about how the employees think and feel is an inward goal and, like most inward goals, it is futile and self destructive.

This is, I recognize, a harsh-sounding thing to say. But leading your business with an outwardly looking perspective is, at least in my experience, the best way to keep your employees motivated and happy.

It is one of the lovely ironies of life—we can never be happy by trying to be so. Happiness comes when we are focused on the happi-

**SPECIFIC TRAITS OF
GOOD LEADERS:**

Integrity
Authenticity
Powerful Communicator
Accessible
Strong Listener
Flexible
Builder Of Teams

*The above traits were published in
The Chief Executive and brain-
stormed by the following leaders:
John Alexander, President and CEO of
the Center For Creative Leadership;
Douglas McCormick, CEO of iVillage;
and Robert Bunker, CEO of Aperture

ness of others. This principle applies to business. Our employees are happiest not when we focus on them, but when we lead them to focus on our products and our customers.

This doesn't mean that you should be insensitive to employees' working conditions, health benefits, fringe benefits and compensation. My rule on that: give as much as you can. Having a healthy business means retaining good people and if you are always losing good employees to the competition then you will never be a truly healthy company. So treat your employees as well or better than your competition. But don't think that will make them happy.

Happiness will come, but only when you persuade them to care about your customers and your work.

SO, HOW DOES ONE BECOME A LEADER AT WORK?

Here's an example from my experience. I'm thinking of a friend of mine who has built a successful business largely by getting very smart and talented people to work very hard for him. He isn't, by conventional standards, an inspiring guy. He doesn't make heart-stirring speeches or send out motivational memos. In fact, he hardly raises his voice. But, what he does do is talk a lot about the quality of good ideas—and he allows his best people plenty of freedom to develop them.

If you work in an environment where good thinking is valued and the freedom to develop ideas is fostered, you are very likely to feel good about what you do. And if you feel good about what you do, you will work hard and smart.

Another example that comes to mind is a colleague, a publisher who has an entirely different leadership style. He is much more hands-on and dogmatic. Yet he gives his people the same thing: The feeling that what they are doing is good and worthwhile. In his case, it is less about creativity and more about quality. His employees feel—and with some justification—that the products they produce are better than most of those they compete against. This kind of feeling can fuel a long and productive career.

You can cultivate the ability to make people believe in your projects and your customers with amazing results. Start today by doing the following 4 things:

1. Think about why you are in business (besides acquiring wealth—which is sensible, but not inspirational). What good does your product/service do? How does it help your customers? Distill it all down to a phrase, if possible (ETR's purpose, for example is to help you become independent and successful.)
2. Ratchet that phrase up a notch by making it more ambitious. (ETR is the best self-help program in the world, because it provides proven advice in daily, digestible doses.)
3. Communicate that idea to your key people. Do it now, by memo, and every time you can in the future.
4. Prove your commitment to the idea by spending time and money on it.

Every month ask yourself "Do I give those around me the feeling that what we're doing is good and worthwhile?" "Do I feel that what I am doing is good and worthwhile?"

If the answers to these questions aren't "yes," come back to the above exercise.

MYTH #4 GOOD BUSINESS = TEAMWORK

Business work as teamwork is a popular idea today.

And in my experience there is a good deal of merit to it, but only in the right time and place. An article by Michael Finley in *Across the Board* magazine entitled "All for One, but None for All," correctly points out that most business is *not* teamwork and most business managers are not team players.

You have risen to the ranks of leadership because you like to be in charge and get things done, not because you like to cooperate. Good leaders understand that teamwork doesn't work in every project. However, teamwork does play an important role, and according to Finley, some leaders have to overcome their "natural resistance" to it.

I agree, and I recommend using teamwork only for defined projects. Projects that have specific goals and definite deadlines. Like hitting a certain sales target, or getting a new product manufactured.

For this kind of objective, you'll do best if you can organize your crew into a team. Remember to let them know the goal and the deadline. Make it clear that everyone is expected to contribute on an individual basis but that the goal is to be accomplished (and enjoyed) as a group.

MYTH #5 CONSIDER "EMOTIONAL INTELLIGENCE" TO GET YOUR PEOPLE TO WORK BETTER.

According to a Gallup poll of 300,000 businesses, between 50% and 60% of employees are not doing their best work. And in a new book called *Follow This Path*, authors Curt Coffman and Gabriel Molina-Gonzales say they have a solution.[2] They recommend leaders consider emotional intelligence and inspire better work by encouraging employees to:

• Buy into your goals.
• Get excited about the business's future.
• Feel as if they are an important part of the program.

You can get a start, the book argues, by having your people respond to the following statements:

---

2 Coffman, Curt, Gonzalez-Molina, Gabriel *Follow this Path: How the World's Greatest Organizations Drive Growth by Unleashing Human Potential*, Warner Books, October 8, 2002.

1. "I know what work is expected of me."
2. "I have the materials and equipment I need to do my work."
3. "I have the opportunity to do what I do best every day."
4. "In the past week, I have been praised for doing good work."
5. "My supervisor or someone else at work seems to care about me as a person."
6. "Someone at work encourages my development."
7. "My opinion seems to count."
8. "My company's mission makes me feel my job is important."
9. "I have a best friend at work."
10. "In the past six months, someone at work has talked to me about my progress."
11. "I have had opportunities to learn and grow at work."

Hmm. I am quite sure that 50% to 60% of the employees I know are not working at their optimum level. And it would be interesting to put these statements to them however, I'm not sure what I could do with that information. I certainly wouldn't want to focus the company's energy on the emotional satisfaction of its disgruntled employees. Disgruntled people are usually unhappy because that's the way they want to be.

Effective managers would rather have happy employees than miserable ones, but they know—from experience if not from intuition—that you don't get happy by trying to be happy.

Instead, professional happiness comes by working hard on a worthwhile goal.

And what about the other 40% to 50%, the motivated, productive employees? Instead, I believe I should be spending my time with them and finding out how I can make their jobs easier.

Something else to note, none of the successful companies I've ever worked with has asked such questions.

MYTH # 6 CONSENSUS BUILDING IS IMPORTANT

Contrary to what some business gurus say, consensus decisions aren't usually better than individual ones. Acquiring a consensus is an inward-looking objective—it solves the wrong problem. It answers the question "What solution can I get everyone to live with?" rather than "What solution is best for the long-term health of the business?"

Consensus makers are politicians. They focus on group dynamics, on finding ideas that please people.

Great business leaders are not politicians at all. In fact, the political instinct is almost opposite of the business instinct.

A good leader wants to identify the best decision and then sell that decision to the key movers and shakers in his division. By focusing on establishing a working quorum—a select support group with the power to make the idea work—he will succeed.

By being selective in building a base, the successful leader gets his ideas realized quickly and without the negative fallout that would come if he tried to build a general consensus.

"Good business" myths like consensus building can be dangerous for business, and I'm not the only one who understands this. So does management and leadership consultant Dave Anderson.

In his book entitled *No-Nonsense Leadership* he wrote about four other business myths worth picking apart here:[3]

MYTH #7: EMPLOYEES WANT TO BECOME EMPOWERED.

In my experience this is simply not true. Most employees want to enjoy their work, earn a good living and spend their spare time and energy on other things—their families, their vacations, their hobbies. It is the rare employee that wants power. When you find one, by all means empower him. Teach him, train him, promote him and empower him. He will become your strongest ally and the foundation of your future. But he, as I say, will be the exception.

Empowerment, in other words, works great with people who want power and not so great with people who don't. Most people—I think you'll find if you pay attention to what they really do and not at what they say—don't want power, but leadership. The bottom line is this: Give people as much power as they want but don't force power on

---

3 Anderson, Dave, *No-Nonsense Leadership: Real World Strategies To Maximize Personal & Corporate Potential*, Creative Broadcast Concepts, November 1, 2001.

those who don't want it and won't accept it.

In this case particularly, instead of power, think about courage. Good leaders inspire courage in their followers. For instance, it has been said that Napoleon had a way of talking and carrying himself that inspired extraordinary bravery. In fact, according to the Duke of Wellington, "the mere presence of Napoleon on the battlefield" made his soldiers braver and stronger. In business, good leaders know how to foster in their employees the confidence and courage to persist and make ideas happen despite difficulty.

MYTH #8: MICROMANAGING IS UNPRODUCTIVE AND DISPIRITING.

There are two big problems with micromanaging: First it takes up a lot of your time that should be spent on more important things. Second it disables the person you are managing.

That said there are times when you have to do it. New hires have to be micromanaged for a period of time. And so do experienced employees when you ask them to do new work, important new work that only you understand.

Strive always to avoid micromanaging but recognize that sometimes, despite your best efforts to the contrary, you'll have to do it. One helpful hint: If you hire exceptional people, they will need only the most modest amount of micromanaging and only in the very beginning.

MYTH #9: A GOOD LEADER NEVER GIVES UP ON HIS EMPLOYEES.

You don't have enough time and your business doesn't have enough money to salvage a bad employee. Even mediocre employees can drag your business into unprofitability.

It's the toughest thing to do, but it will give you the best results—get rid of the bad employees. Jack Welch said he routinely fired the weakest fifth of his employees at General Electric. You should too. It won't be pleasant but it will make a world of difference.

MYTH #10: EMPLOYEES NEED TO BE GIVEN TANGIBLE REWARDS FOR THEIR HARD WORK: EXTRA PAY, BETTER BENEFITS, A NICER OFFICE, AND OTHER FRINGE BENEFITS.

It sounds nice but you can't bribe people to work better. How they work is a matter of deeply ingrained habits, habits that are not likely to change because of any incentive you throw in front of them.

That being said, if you practice the skill of good leadership you can inspire people to support your objectives. Remember, what I said in the introduction: the act of inspiring, which is gentle and uplifting, will always work better than the less elegant techniques of persuasion such as badgering and bullying and bribing. And you'll feel better in the end too.

I'm not saying you shouldn't reward your employees. You should pay attention to your top performers. Compliment them when they do well and correct them when they err. Your growing approval of their increasing skillfulness and the opportunities that brings will be their most happy reward.

To become a leader is to become powerful and important. To become a leader is to put yourself in a position of authority and influence. To become a leader is a responsibility and a privilege. It is something that can change your life faster and further than just about anything else you can learn to do. And the most successful way of getting all of your people to work for you is to create a compelling, worthwhile vision and inspire them with the work itself. Much of the material in the coming chapters will show you how. Do this and you WILL become a great leader.

CHAPTER 2:
LEADING SOMETIMES MEANS FOLLOWING

"What must leaders do to ensure results?" More than ever before in history, the answer lies in following—following our vision and purpose, following our principles for managing toward that purpose, and following all the people who will make an organization's vision happen."
~ Douglas K. Smith, from *The Leader of The Future*[4]

One of the most important leadership lessons I ever learned was revealed to me under the most unlikely of circumstances: I was dancing. I had reluctantly agreed to take ballroom dance lessons with my wife. The wonderful thing about ballroom dancing is that there is no ambiguity about leadership—unlike marriage.

Modern marriage is based on the idea of partnership. One partner is in charge of some things and the other partner of other things. Reasonable partners will divide up the workload according to abili-

---

4 Smith, Douglas K. contributor in *The Leader of the Future*, The Drucker Foundation, New York: 1996.

ties, inclinations, etc and this will result in a sensible and productive division of labor. That is, as far as I can tell, the official and correct view of things. As is the valuation of labors: what each partner does is to be valued equally.

That was the deal when I got married—way back in the beginning of the modern period. But being a creature of the old world I secretly believed that the things I was in charge of were more important than the things my wife was in charge of. This perspective of superiority allowed me to rest comfortably in a partnering relationship—a relationship, I must admit, that has never been my favorite.

I admit it. I like to be in charge. And for most of my life I have ended up being in charge. This is why I think I'm qualified to talk about leadership. It's also why I was very unsuited to the modern, partnership marriage. I wanted to be in charge!

What happened was very typical of most marriages of my generation. Without ever saying so explicitly, my wife allowed me the fantasy of being in charge of the important things but bit by bit over the years I found that the actual decision-making pattern changed. Whereas in the beginning it seemed like I could make the final decisions about a lot of things, in the end the only thing I was left in charge of was the remote control. And that was only after we got rid of the television.

As an old friend of mine puts it, "When my wife and I got married, we were both sergeants. Twenty years later, she's a general while I'm still a sergeant. I don't know how she got promoted, but she did."

I don't want you to think that I suffered mutely during this transition from equality to complete-and-total subordination. I protested every step of the way. I still wanted to be in charge and was always disappointed when the general would contradict my order. This continued until we started taking ballroom dance lessons.

WHAT YOU CAN LEARN ABOUT
LEADERSHIP FROM BALLROOM DANCE

In ballroom dance, like business, one person leads and the other person follows. And if one person is a man and the other a woman, guess who gets to lead? Yes, in ballroom dancing—even today—the man leads. This is a flagrant contradiction— not only of the course of a marriage but also of common sense. After all, your wife can dance. And you look (and feel) ridiculous on the dance floor. No matter. Tradition rules in this rare world. You may move like Steve Martin in "The Jerk," but you are in charge of the dance.

"It usually comes as quite a shock," our dance instructor explained to us that first day, "but if you stick with it, it can work." Needless to say, I was delighted to find out that in this particular circumstance, without any discussion or equivocation whatsoever, I was going to be the leader. For my lovely dance partner, however, it was a different story. Taking a following role—and not just a following role but also one that does not resist the direction of the leader—well, this was difficult for her. (It might have been especially hard because this involved locomotion —as in driving the family car.)

More than once, my dance partner broke down in mid-lesson. "I don't think I can do this!" she said in a voice that sent chills down my spine. "Learning to follow," our instructor said sympathetically, "is not easy. It's a skill. And for some people, it's a difficult one. For one thing, you have to do the same thing your partner is doing except backward. Just as important, you have to follow his lead even if it seems as if he's going the wrong way."

Oh, how I loved hearing that explanation. And each time our instructor said it—and I assure you he had to repeat it dozens of times during the course of our lessons—it was sweet music to my ears. Finally, happily, justly . . . I was in charge!

STRONG LEADERS DON'T DISCOUNT THEIR FOLLOWERS

But soon after that first triumph I learned something else about dancing, something that made me realize that moving around the ballroom floor was going to take more thought and (dare I say it?) sensitivity than I imagined. After a month or so of getting the basics down, and just as I was picking up confidence and really starting to swing my partner; our instructor began to bring my dancing to a whole new level.

"You can't just throw her around like a rag doll," he explained one afternoon. You can't expect her to follow your lead when you give her no fair warning of what you are going to do and then suddenly yank her in some unforeseeable direction." I couldn't? Why not? I was the boss! I was the leader.

That's when he showed me how it feels to be poorly led. He made me assume my wife's role. "Now I'll show you how you are leading," he said. What followed wasn't, as they say, pretty. It was much closer to Greco-Roman wrestling than ballroom dancing. Needless to say, I got the point.

"Following takes a great deal of skill," he said. "But so does leading. Leading is not just about moving in the direction you want to go. It's about having the proper frame, and holding your partner the proper way and moving in the proper sequence so that when you do decide to move she is prepared and the movement doesn't damage her."

That night I spent some time mulling over my beliefs about leadership. Up until then I had done very well bossing around my employees pretty much the way I bossed around my wife on the dance floor. Now—having had the opportunity to feel the physical affect of that sort of approach—I began to reconsider my tactics.

Yes, you could get "things done" that way. I could propel my wife from one point on the dance floor to another. But the result of this sort of dancing had several undesirable results. For one thing, my wife didn't enjoy dancing with me. And I didn't want that. For another thing, we didn't look as graceful as I had imagined. I just wasn't as good at dancing as I thought I was. Could the same be true of the way I had danced through business?

The question was rhetorical. I recognized that although I had accomplished a great deal by bossing my way around, I might have injured some people along the way. Just as bad, or worse—but certainly more surprising—I had probably achieved less than I could have otherwise. I got the job done, but less efficiently and in a brutish sort of way.

Traditional businesses, like traditional dancing, do not follow the

3 SECRETS OF HIGHLY EFFECTIVE LEADERSHIP

You can be successful by simply throwing your weight in the direction you want to go and pushing or yanking your followers with you. Or you can learn the secrets of leadership and arrive at your destination sooner, with a better result and with a happier and more willing-to-accomplish-the-next-mission team.

I learned 3 secrets about leadership from my instructor. To be an effective leader you must have:

1. Knowledge. You must know what you are doing. If you don't, you are being unfair to your partner.
2. Preparation. You must think about what you are going to do—plan it thoughtfully—before you do it. You can't expect your partner to follow your lead if your lead is weak or confused because you're making a decision at the last moment.
3. Awareness. You must know where your partner is at all times. Sometimes, your partner may be out of step. That doesn't give you a reason to step on her toe. A good leader is always completely aware of his partner's position at all times.

partnership paradigm. Traditional businesses are hierarchical, and they work better that way. Moreover, in a traditional business, the boss has the right to hire and fire his employees, which makes "being in charge" and leading that much easier. But in business, as in dancing, being in charge is not the end of it. The purpose of business is to provide value in a marketplace for a profit. Doing that requires a great many skills, not the least of which is the skill of leadership.

Leadership means persuading people to follow you. And doing that means you have to be willing to lead. You have to know what you want to accomplish and how to get there. You also need to know where your employees are at any point in time—not their feet so much (though that's important), but their heads. And just like becoming a good ballroom dancer, becoming a good leader takes practice.

The main reason new managers fail in their leadership is not necessarily due to lack of skill, it's due to lack of support. In contrast, a successful leader knows how to build a network of support from the moment he or she walks in the office on the first day. This network is the foundation of success. To build a network like this you must meet with subordinates and learn from them about the organization's weaknesses. Formulate a plan that puts the interests of the organization and the your superior first, not your own interests.

CHAPTER 3:
WHY NEW MANAGERS FAIL:
THE MOST COMMON LEADERSHIP PITFALLS

"There are only two forces that unite men—fear and interest."
~Napoleon Bonaparte, *Military Maxims*, 1804-15

A report I read recently said four out of 10 new managers fail in their first year. The report claimed the primary reason was lack of support. This corresponds to my own experience.

When you take over a new job, you will encounter some enthusiastic support, but mostly you'll find skepticism, cautious cooperation, and in some cases outright resistance. This will come from all quarters, from your new employees, your new supervisor, your new clients, and even the "outside" world of vendors, support staff, and/or consultants.

You can make the transition easier and more productive and still be seen in a positive way, if you follow 8 simple guidelines.

Set Up Individual Meetings

First, understand the best way to handle the situation is to come in slowly. Before you do or say anything, make individual appointments with everybody whose cooperation could help you. This should include all of your staff members. Invite each person to sit down with you for a short, informal chat.

Be Kind

When you meet with someone, make an effort to put him at ease. Start by saying at least one positive thing about him. It can be something you've heard about his abilities, such as "I hear you're a wizard at getting our suppliers to work for you." If you can't come up with anything else say something semi-personal, such as "I like that tie."

Ask A Lot of Questions

Ask questions. Ask about the business generally, his department, his supervisor, his colleagues, and (if applicable) his employees. This will give you material to use later on to say something positive to the other people you're going to be talking to. Ask him what he likes best about his work and what he could live without. Ask his opinion about something that has "been on your mind."

Listen

Let him do most of the talking. This will accomplish several objectives: It will make his feel, if nothing else, that you are a good conversationalist. (Although it may surprise you, the person who asks questions and says very little is usually thought of as a good conversationalist.) It will give him a chance to vent his frustrations, which might help him down the road to trusting you. And it will give you a lot of good information. In fact, during this conversation it's a good idea to take notes for reference later on. You'll be surprised at how much good stuff you'll get. Every time I've been in this situation, I've found people not only willing, but actually bursting to tell an "outsider" all of the company scuttlebutt.

Very important: At this first meeting, make no judgments and say absolutely nothing about anyone else. At this point in time, anything you say will probably be held against you.

Send Out A Thank You Memo

When you've completed all of the interviews, send out a simple memo—a handwritten one is best—thanking each person for his thoughts. Each memo should mention some specific comment he made that you found "helpful." If you have taken some notes as you should have, you'll have plenty to mention here.

Think About What You Want To Do

Then, spend some time thinking about how you want to proceed. Talk to trusted friends and advisers. Get some feedback, but keep it between you and your outside, confidential world. When you are sure you know what needs to be done, you can take action.

Explain Your Plans To Your Supervisor

Before you do anything, you'll have to explain your plans to your new supervisor. And you'll have to do that in a very diplomatic way. Yes you want to impress him with your good judgment and willingness to move forward, but more importantly you'll want to make him feel very comfortable that your interest is in making things work better for HIM, not you.

Talk To Everyone Affected

When it comes time to implement the changes, call in the affected people individually, if feasible, and tell them what you intend to do and why. On rare occasions, this is not possible. Most of the time, however, it can be arranged. Be sure to tell each person how he will benefit from the change, even if it means he will be free to find a better job. Before the discussion ends, ask each person to summarize the conversation to make sure he understands what was said.

If you can do all of this, you will be well on your way to being seen as a strong leader in your new organization. But as you begin to establish relationships with the people who work for you there's another pitfall to be wary of, one many managers can't seem to avoid.

Be Friendly, Not Friends

Remember to always be fair and friendly but never forget that your primary relationship is one based on business. You do neither yourself nor others a favor by trying to be friends.

Don't dump your problems on them. It doesn't matter how stressed out you are. And it matters less how open and understanding an employee is. There is no good reason to tell him your problems. He is not responsible for them, nor is he in charge of making you feel better. Be pleasant and keep your troubles to yourself. And don't allow your employees to dump their problems on you. It may make you feel like a hero to provide the solution, but it robs them of the opportunity to learn how to fend for themselves.

And you should be cautioned with leaning to far the other way too and falling victim to yet another pitfall: suffering the consequences of having a sharp tongue.

Don't Hurt People's Feelings

Ambitious entrepreneurs and corporate climbers are equally capable of focusing so intensely on their business goals that other considerations, like feelings, get sacrificed. I'm guilty of this. In fact, it's practically my style. I am impatient, critical, condescending, or combative—anything to get the result I seek. I excuse my behavior by blaming my victims. They are too slow, too dumb, too careless, or too lazy.

There is no question that in the short run, I accomplish more with threats, rebukes, and criticism than I do by making nice. Over time, however, my behavior comes back to haunt me. The feelings I hurt vibrate long after my pleasure in venting has dissipated. What I end up with is a lot of invisible stuff working against me.

Moral Of The Story, Don't Be A Bastard

As you climb the ladder of success, you are going to bump into some slow-moving, not-moving, and backward-moving fellow climbers. How you get around them will determine both how high you climb and how good you feel about yourself.

When I find myself slipping into that old familiar pattern I try to follow the example set by an extremely successful friend and colleague of mine who has never, as far as I know, said a mean word to anyone. When confronted by monumentally stupid ideas or bad performances, he is careful, even gentle, in his comments. He never yells.

7 GUIDELINES TO HELP YOU SUCCEED AS A LEADER

- Recognize that another person's laziness, lack of ambition, clumsiness, and incompetence are not intended to harm you. They existed before you came into the picture. Be compassionate.
- Be compassionate but not accepting. You set the standards. Make them fair. Make them clear. But expect them to be met.
- The moment you recognize that someone will not improve, make the decision to replace him. Do so with kindness.
- Ask, don't tell.
- Listen before you speak.
- Say something good before you say something bad.
- Be careful in your criticism.

He never scolds. He simply makes suggestions or asks questions. As a result, he has few enemies, even among his competitors.

When he is presented with a one-sided proposition, he will say something like, "Gee, I don't think I can afford that," rather than, "How can you even suggest that, you greedy, self-centered son-of-a-bitch?"

When he sees bad writing, he might ask, "Do you think this headline is as specific as it could be?" rather than say, "You are hopeless. You can't even write a simple headline. Never cast your shadow in my office again!"

If you are one of the nice few, your challenge will be to overcome your tendency to put up with slow movers, but if you're more like me, you'll need to make some changes.

The truth is; it is never NECESSARY to mistreat people. If you can rely on good leadership skills, you'll never have to say an abrupt word.

$\left[\textbf{KEY POINT}\right]$

Creative problem solving, or thinking "out of the box" is an essential characteristic of strong leaders. You can learn to be a creative problem solver and think "out of the box" by moving past any assumptions, rules or guidelines you have about the problem or issue.

CHAPTER 4:
THINKING "OUT OF THE BOX"—WHAT IT *REALLY* MEANS

"We do not at present educate people to think but, rather, to have opinions, and that is something altogether different."
—Louis L 'Amour, *Education of a Wandering Man*, 1989[5]

For a while now the management experts have been talking about the need to think "out of the box" to view problems and challenges from a fresh perspective. Most of the time you don't need to— a conventional approach to business works just fine.

But when problems get especially difficult or when you find yourself in unfamiliar territory, thinking out of the box is not only helpful, it's necessary. Unfortunately, very few leaders actually do it. In fact, of the hundreds of successful business people I know, fewer than a dozen have this valuable skill. In this chapter you'll learn how you can use "out of the box" thinking to your advantage.

FIRST, A LITTLE HISTORY

The phrase "thinking out of the box" originated with an intelli-

5 L 'Amour, Louis, *Education of a Wandering Man*, Bantam Books: Reissue 1989

gence test called the Nine-Dot Box.[6] You've probably seen it. Imagine three rows of three dots, each equally spaced some distance apart on a plain piece of paper. The challenge is to connect the dots by drawing a minimum number of lines. The only rules: that you must draw a line through every dot once and only once, all lines must be straight (no curves), and your pen/pencil cannot leave the paper.

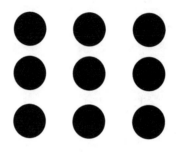

If you've ever seen this done as a "bar trick," you know that most people cannot figure out how to do it with fewer than five lines. Yet, it's quite easy to do it with four. And it's even possible to do it with one.

Most people can't solve the puzzle because they think, mistakenly, that they are not allowed to draw the line beyond the perimeters of the box. Those who realize they can draw their lines "out of the box," are able to connect all of the dots with four or fewer lines. (One way to do this is to roll the paper into a cylinder with all of the dots lining up and then connect them with one line.)

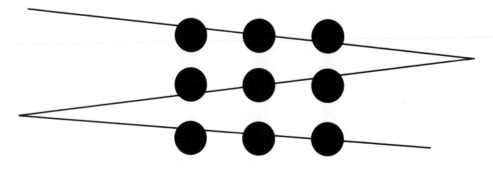

---

6 Phrase Finder, http://phrasefinder.co.uk

LEARNING TO THINK "OUT OF THE BOX"

The conventional way of teaching yourself to think "out of the box" involves questions. When stuck with a seemingly unsolvable problem ask yourself, "Am I making any unfounded assumptions? And "Is there a way of doing this by breaking any rules?"

If asking the questions doesn't help then make a list of all the assumptions and restrictions you "think" you are operating on and within. Sometimes, simply by seeing one of these in print, an idea about how to go beyond the problem will pop into your head.

I recently used "out of the box" thinking to resolve a stalemate

ANOTHER WAY TO STIMULATE CREATIVE THINKING . . . BUILD A MIND MAP™

Mindmapping™ was created by Tony Buzan and is based on the thinking and note taking styles of many of history's greatest brains including Charles Darwin, Michelangelo, Leonardo da Vinci and Mark Twain. Don't let that intimidate you though, it's quite simple. You see, it allows your brain to think in the way it was created too . . . following a networked, branching structure. Here's how to do it:

Step 1: Get some colorful marker—highlighters are perfect—a pen and a sheet of paper. Take the paper and lay it out horizontally in front of you. Draw a symbol or a picture in the center of your page. The picture should be representative of the topic for the mind map . . . it can be as simple as a circle or as elaborate as you want it to be.

Step 2: Now think about the topic you're trying to come up with new ideas for or about. What key words are associated with it? Print them (single words only!) on lines radiating from your central image. Remember to print on the lines. If you feel like using an image instead of a word, do so. If you get stuck, choose a key word and write down words associated with it on these lines.

Step 3: When you feel you have as many ideas as you can come up with, look for relationships between the words that will help you organize your ideas. Look for words that you've written again and again, these are normally important themes.

Step 4: Then connect the related words with arrows, codes, asterisks and colors. Eliminate elements that aren't related to your purpose. Then put the remaining branches (lines with words) in a sequence using numbers or by redrawing the mind map in a clock wise order. You should start coming up with all kinds of original, spontaneous ideas. You'll see connections between things that used to seem completely separate. This gives you a clear view of the big picture and encourages big thinking!

The above mind mapping™ process was taken from Michael J. Gelb's book, Thinking For A Change.[7] If you'd like to learn more about mind mapping™, pick up a copy of Tony Buzan's book, Mind Map Book: How To Use Radiant Thinking to Maximize Your Brain's Untapped Potential.[8]

between two friends and business partners. They were deadlocked on a contract that was working well for one but not the other. The former wanted the stipulations of the contract honored verbatim. "You agreed to them," he said. "And you should live with them. The other believed that the contract, although signed, was no longer reasonable. "I can't agree to it because it's just not fair," he said.

There were several unspoken assumptions operating here. One was the assumption that if the partner who didn't want to "honor" the contract was allowed to break it, he would prove to be an untrustworthy partner. Another was that by asking that the letter of the contract be honored the first partner was proving himself unreasonable and so would be unreasonable in the future. Both assumptions were understandable, but both—I knew because I knew these two guys—were wrong.

I solved the problem by focusing on a third assumption—that the

7 Gelb, Michael J. *Thinking For A Change: Discovering The Power To Create, Communicate, and Lead,* Crown Publishers: New York: 1995.
8 Buzan, Barry, Buzan, Tony, *Mind Map Book: How To Use Radiant Thinking to Maximize Your Brain's Untapped Potential,* Plume: March 1996,

contract itself was the basis of the relationship. I pointed out to each of them that their relationship was a long one and had always been both fair and trustworthy before. They each agreed. "What you can trust, I pointed out, is that you are both have a similar idea of what is "fair." And I proved that by pointing out that the first partner—the one who wanted the contract honored to the letter—acknowledged it wasn't fair.

"Trust in your experience of each other," I suggested. "Recognize that you each have both a similar idea about what is fair and a commitment to honesty. That is what your business is based on, not a stupid piece of paper that can be violated anyway."

They realized they couldn't afford to litigate and that litigation would only make things worse. More importantly, they had a chance to see their relationship from "outside the box" and saw that is was a bigger and better relationship than they had imagined. The incident was resolved and now they have a better working relationship—and are making more money together—than ever.

The next time you run into a difficult problem, think about the hidden assumptions that might restrict the way you approach a solution—and ignore them. You'll be surprised by how easily and often this works. Before long, you'll be known as a creative problem solver.

Creative leadership focuses on the big picture. This is why creative leaders are stronger in every sense than reactive leaders. Creative leaders are long-term oriented, never care where they stand in any pecking order, focus solely on providing better products and services—this is what it's all about. They ask themselves: What do my potential customers need now? How can I make our current customers happier? How can we make the products we sell them better?

CHAPTER 5:
CREATIVE V.S. REACTIVE LEADERSHIP

"Shallow men believe in luck . . . Strong men believe in cause and effect."
~Ralph Waldo Emerson, *The Conduct of Life*[9]

In the last chapter I talked about *how* to think "out of the box." This kind of innovative thinking is an essential element of the most effective leadership style: creative leadership. You'll hear business experts throw this term around a lot. But what does it mean really? According to the *Executive Leadership Newsletter*, leaders practicing creative leadership focus on the big picture.

I like to think of creative leadership as open leadership versus reactive or *closed* leadership. For example, a creative leader is long-term oriented, people-friendly and loyal, eager to provide better products and service. A creative leader is unconcerned about where he stands in just about any pecking order—in the industry or within the business. On the other hand, reactive leaders are short-term oriented. They need to have all of the answers and want to make decisions per-

---

9 Emerson, Ralph Waldo, *The Conduct of Life*, University Press of the Pacific; April 2002.

sonally. Reactive leaders only motivate their people sporadically and don't inspire growth in their people or in their business—growth that's needed to achieve a high level of success.

Reactive leadership won't get you far in business. It's simply counterproductive. The purpose of business is to provide value in a marketplace for a profit. Doing that requires a great many skills, not the least of which is strong, creative leadership.

FOLLOW THE EXAMPLE SET BY THE BEST LEADERS

You can improve your abilities as a creative leader by doing what

A recent issue of Executive Leadership Newsletter broke down the characteristics of creative and reactive leaders into a list. Which ones apply to you?

CHARACTERISTICS OF CREATIVE LEADERS

- internally driven
- focused on the work, not politics
- oriented around goals, not crises
- good at building good relationships
- uses strongest talents to the fullest
- sets aggressive long-term goals

CHARACTERISTICS OF REACTIVE LEADERS

- motivated by external factors like money and power.
- focused on corporate politics, not the work.
- allow their time to be dictated by what's in their inbox.
- sometimes ignore their strongest talents in favor of "good management."
- plan in one- to five-year increments.
- believe nothing is sacred and relationships are expendable.[10]

Practice the characteristics of creative leaders. If you see some of the characteristics of reactive leaders in your leadership style recognize them and ignore them.

10 Executive Leadership Newsletter (ETR folks hopefully have full citation)

COMMON PHRASES OR BELIEFS THAT ARE ROADBLOCKS TO CREATIVE LEADERSHIP:

"If that were such a good idea, someone would have already done it."

"The lawyers won't like it."

"Don't rock the boat."

"We're not ready for that kind of change."

"Yes, but . . . "

"If it ain't broke don't fix it."

"You have to prove that it will work before we try anything."

"It's not in the budget."

"We've always done it this way."

Michael J. Gelb author of Thinking For A Change[11], calls these "bunkerisms," He says the classic TV show character Archie Bunker used to respond to creative suggestions with a similar phrase, "Stifle yourself." Don't let your leadership fall victim to this kind of resistance!

the best business leaders do. In my experience, these men and women are always asking themselves the following questions:

1. What do potential customers need now? What worries them? What would they be eager to buy?
2. How can I make our current customers happier?
3. How can we make the products we sell them better? How can we make them more useful? How can we make them more valuable?

Start asking yourself these questions on a regular basis. They will not only stimulate your creative juices but they'll help you stay focused on the big picture. And you'll find your answers will help you advance your business like never before.

---

11 Gelb, Michael J. *Thinking For A Change: Discovering The Power To Create, Communicate, and Lead,* Crown Publishers: New York: 1995.

Strong leaders are effective decision makers. They can assess a situation, see beyond preconceived notions and prejudices, seek proper advice, and make a decision within a set time frame.

CHAPTER 6:
MAKING DIFFICULT DECISIONS EASY: A 7 STEP PLAN

"Nothing is more difficult, and therefore more precious, than to be able to decide."
~Napoleon Bonaparte

There are many skills and talents you don't need to lead but one thing you have to do is make decisions. It could be said that the success of a leader is entirely dependent on the decisions he makes. And if you think about the key decisions—what direction your enterprise should take, who its key actors should be how much risk to take, etc.—it's clear that making good decisions matters.

Why is it then that there are so many bad decisions being made in business? According to William Altier, author of *The Thinking Man's Toolbox: Effective Processes for Problem Solving and Decision Making*, it's because of the decision maker's closeness to the problem. Altier explains that a manager's existing beliefs and perceptions about the situation handicaps his ability to decide well.

He says most managers just can't seem to approach a problem with an open mind. "An excellent thinker," Altier says, must be able to "digest the information presented and separate the relevant from the irrelevant, and come to logical conclusions regardless of any prior knowledge about a situation or any perceptions, pet ideas or biases."[12]

Although prejudices will always exist, Altier says a skilled thinker learns to control them. I couldn't agree more. Good decision making requires intelligence, experience and judgment—especially when it comes to making difficult decisions. These are difficult *not* because of the decision itself, but because of your fears over making the wrong choice or even worse, concerns that your decision will result in a terrible mistake that will cost you new opportunities for success.

To overcome these fears and any preconceived notions you have you need to establish a process for making decisions. There are certain practical techniques you can use to immeasurably improve your ability to make sound decisions. Here are the 7 steps I recommend:

STEP 1: ASSESS THE SITUATION AND SET A "THINKING" DEADLINE

When faced with any decision it's imperative to size up the situation and examine it from all angles before doing anything else. In *The Thinking Man's Tool Box*, Altier calls this first step of any decision making process "situation assessment." The idea is to gather information and think with an open mind. If you remind yourself to do this it really works. Don't be lazy though. Don't be satisfied with just those solutions that come quickly and easily.

And don't misunderstand me here either. You don't have a license to think about a single decision for weeks upon weeks. You should think, but do it in a timely fashion. This couldn't be more important in business as most decisions have time constraints. If you wait around your opportunity could be gone.

I find it helpful to create a deadline for my thinking. I usually base the amount of time I spend assessing a decision on the importance of the thing being decided. For example, last week one of the businesses I work with was hit with a serious law suit, one that threatened not just the profitability of the company but its livelihood. The management was in a panic. All sorts of ideas were thrown about—legal,

---

12 Altier, William J. *The Thinking Man's Toolbox: Effective Processes for Problem Solving and Decision Making*, New York: Oxford University Press, 1999.

structural and cash flow responses to the threat. Since so much weighed in the balance each decision needed to be right. Yet action needed to be taken.

We adopted a strategy that put off all decisions till Friday. From Monday till Friday we would meet every day and discuss options and review recommendations.

In between meetings everyone would think about what was suggested and do whatever research was needed. The five-day assessment period, coupled with a fixed deadline, was just the sort of parameters we needed to come to a sure and confident set of decisions. Had we tried to decide everything the first day we would have made a few serious mistakes. Had we not set a deadline we would have put off the decisions until it was too late.

That's what I recommend you do, especially during crises. First figure out what deadlines, if any, you have. Then determine how much time you can devote to deliberating in order to meet those deadlines.

By scheduling your assessment and deciding time out in advance you'll achieve an immediate sense of order amid chaos and you'll give yourself the best possible chance of making all the right choices.

Note: when assessing problems make sure you don't confuse a problem's *symptoms* for the actual problem itself. For example, a shortage of money is only a symptom of poor spending habits or too much debt, it's not the problem). When it comes time to deal with a major problem in your business make sure that everyone talks about both symptoms and causes.

STEP 2: FIGURE OUT WHAT YOU WANT

According to an editorial I saw in *The Economist*, any business strategy should answer two basic questions, "Where do you want to go?" and "How do you want to get there?"[13] Your strategy for making important decisions should do the same.

It's not always easy to answer these two questions. If you get stuck or are unsure, try asking other, more specific questions such as:

---

13 "Making Strategy," *The Economist,* 1 March 1997. Quoted by Kathleen M Eisenhardt in "Strategy as Strategic Decision Making," *Sloan Management Review,* Spring 1999.

- "What exact results do I want to achieve by making this decision?"
- "How do these compare to my overall business goals?"
- "What are the benefits and penalties that will follow from making this decision?"
- "Which of those benefits is greatest?"
- "Which of those penalties is too great?"
- "Which goals can I live without?"

Discuss these questions with trusted colleagues. Ask your employees what they think abaout particular issues. Record the results and review them over a period of days.

As recommended above, work within time frames with a definite deadlines. And do your best to think with an open mind and without prejudice.

Another important part of this step is to consider the expense of indecision. If you can't make up your mind and do nothing, what will that cost you?

STEP 3: DECIDE TO DECIDE . . . OR NOT

Difficult decisions are never easy.

And even the best-made ones are never perfect. Accept from the beginning that the solution you come to will be a mixed bag. Aim to make it mostly good. Stick to your deadline. But give yourself the grace of deciding not to decide. Sometimes—and this happens more often than one might expect—it's better to allow some problems to work themselves out.

At several points during the time period you've set for yourself, ask if it might be better to do nothing. Don't do nothing because you can't decide. Consider all the pros and cons of deciding as well as the pros and cons of deciding to do nothing and then choose the path that makes the most sense.

You can always look at the problem at a later date.

Note: there is a big difference between deciding not to do anything and procrastination.

One is the action of a prudent leader. The other, the symptom of a weak one.

STEP 4: DECISION ANALYSIS

So you've decided to decide. Now it's time to consider possible outcomes of what you decide to help you make the best possible choice. Altier calls this step "decision analysis."

Based on the information you've gathered so far, design alternatives and write them down.

Think ahead. Ask yourself "What will happen if . . . ?"

Consider the pros and cons, the risks and rewards of each alternative. Figure out the *worst* possible outcome of any contemplated decision.

Then, figure out the *best* possible outcome.

Be realistic, but be creative when structuring your choices. Combine different ideas and look for new solutions and plans. Again, think with an open mind!

Next, compare your alternatives and weigh their outcomes. It's important to compare these to the goals and priorities you wrote down in step 2. You need to take all of these factors into account to determine your best course of action.

STEP 5: ASK FOR ADVICE

Never be afraid to admit that you need guidance. If you still can't decide, narrow your alternatives down to a small group of choices, and then ask for advice.

Talk to someone you trust, preferably someone who has had to make similarly tough decisions. Sometimes simply the act of talking things through with another can help you quickly determine your best choice.

A second point of view can also help in identifying any preconceived beliefs or judgments you've held about the issue at hand—prejudices that could be blocking you from making a good decision.

And if you're still having trouble deciding, here's a little trick I like to use: ask yourself what decision someone you admire would come to. Sometimes that's all it takes to make your choice clear.

STEP 6: KEEP TO YOUR DECISION DEADLINE

Expect too to feel some mounting pressure to postpone the decision. Often when confronted with complex problems and countless ramifications decision makers are inclined to procrastinate.

Don't do that. Stick to your deadline. If you've set a realistic deadline and performed the above steps in a timely manner you will (and should) have a decision by your deadline date.

Again time is key. Don't make a habit of pushing your deadlines. It's a bad habit to get into and will only hurt you in the long run. Also important is avoiding procrastination. Don't put off getting started on the decision making process. That's a trait that Kathleen Eisenhardt author of "Strategy as Strategic Decision Making"[14] discovered is common in less successful strategic decisions makers.

Eisenhardt spent more than a decade researching decision making and strategizing among top management teams in entrepreneurial firms around the world. She found that the least successful decision makers were often aware of an opportunity or problem but they didn't get around to doing anything about it for months. Of course by that time, they'd missed the boat. Eisenhardt says these managers had two things in common: they let "critical issues languish" or they made "shot gun" strategic choices against hard deadlines.

To avoid falling into this trap you need your deadlines, or what Eisenhardt calls a "decision-making rhythm."[15] If you set deadlines like I do for each part of your decision making process, and follow the same process for every decision, you'll quickly establish a pace. Eisenhardt found it was pace that helped the most effective strategic decision makers plan their progress. They focused on this pace, and not on the speed of their decision making.

Most importantly, when you do finally reach your decision, have confidence! If you've performed the above steps faithfully there's no reason to doubt your choice.

---

14 Eisenhardt, Kathleen M. 'Strategy as Strategic Decision-Making" Sloan Management Review, Spring, 1999.
15 Eisenhardt, Kathleen M. 'Strategy as Strategic Decision-Making" Sloan Management Review, Spring, 1999.

PRACTICE YOUR DECISION MAKING SKILLS

Use these steps for every important decision you make and you'll quickly find your pace. Soon you'll be able to recognize familiar patterns of the decision making process. And you'll make sound decisions more easily in the future. Plus, following this process will help put prejudices that could alter your decision-making skills to the wayside. You'll find yourself thinking bigger, thinking more creatively and effectively—and making better decisions than you ever have before.

So stay positive and don't second-guess yourself.

STEP 7: IMPLEMENT YOUR DECISION

Once you've made your decision, the work's not over though. Now you must take action. Inform everyone affected by your decision. Tell them how they'll be affected and what course of action they need to take.

Managers who are able to make and implement a decision successfully share certain traits according to Eisenhardt. Traits I feel are worth mentioning here. She found they all had a negative view of politicking, seeing it as I do as a "waste of valuable time." Eisenhardt says politicking negatively impacts good decision making because it distorts "the information base." I couldn't agree more. As a decision-maker, as a business leader, you must focus on what's best for the organization, not what's best for an individual—including yourself.

$$\left[\textbf{KEY POINT}\,\right]$$

Relying on facts and details is more important than using gut instinct in lower levels of leadership. However, senior managers must have and be able to use a reliable gut instinct and at the top, your gut instinct is the most valuable thing you have. Leaders trust in their personal experiences more than those of others.

CHAPTER 7:
REASON OR GUT INSTINCT, WHICH RULES?
(SEPARATING THE MEN FROM THE BOYS)

"Well-bred instinct meets reason halfway."
~George Santayana, *The Life of Reason: Reason in Society*, 1905[16]

It has always seemed clear to me that a good gut instinct is worth even more than an MBA from Harvard. So it didn't come as a surprise when I read an article recently in the *Harvard Business Review* supporting my view, it was called "When to Trust Your Gut." According to the author, Alden M. Hayashi, senior editor of the *Harvard Business Review*, "the higher up the corporate ladder people climb, the more they'll need well-honed business instincts." In other words, gut instinct is what separates the men from the boys in business.

THERE IS A PLACE WHERE REASON RULES

In lowlier positions, the tendency to stick to the numbers is often beneficial. Those middle managers who shoot from the hip frequent-

---

16 Santayana, George *The Life of Reason: Reason in Society*, 1905, Dover Publications: Reissue: 1983.

ly make costly mistakes. But those who sharpen their pencils and follow the rules keep the bottom line in black. As you move up the corporate power chain however, problems get more complex and decisions must be made more quickly. Attention to detail becomes relatively less important. And at a certain level of leadership, having a reliable gut instinct is perhaps the most valuable thing.

Ralph S. Larsen, chairman and CEO of Johnson & Johnson, explains the distinction: "Very often, people will do a brilliant job up through the middle-management levels, where it's very heavily quantitative in terms of the decision making. But then they reach senior management, where the problems get more complex and ambiguous, and we discover that their judgment or intuition is not what it should be. And when that happens, it's a problem. It's a big problem."

WHEN GUT INSTINCT IS VITAL

Richard Abdoo, chairman and CEO of Wisconsin Energy Corporation, agrees. He says that as business speeds up and decisions must be made more quickly, this ability is even more important.

But decision making, the experts tell us, is far from a rational and logical process. It involves that emotional charge you get that seems to tell you what to do when your mind is frozen or confused—this is what we call your gut instinct.

THINK FROM YOUR GUT

Henry Mintzberg, professor of management at McGill University and a longtime proponent of intuitive decision making offers an explanation for thinking from the gut. Mintzberg believes that the subconscious mind is continuously processing information that the conscious mind may not be aware of. He says that a sense of revelation (the "Aha!" moment) occurs when the conscious mind finally learns something that the subconscious mind has already known.

Nobel laureate Herbert A. Simon, a professor of psychology and computer science at Carnegie Mellon University offered more insight into this process. Simon believes that experience enables people to "chunk" information so that they can store and retrieve it easily. He says that even the most sophisticated gut judgments can be broken into patterns and rules. In chess, for example, he found that grand masters are able to recognize and recall perhaps 50,000 significant patterns out of the astronomical number of ways in which the various pieces can be arranged on a board.

This stored information is then "cross-indexed." Our brains automatically search and find patterns in one area that correspond to patterns in another. For example, a marketing executive might see something in a health-oriented advertising campaign that subconsciously suggests an idea for a financial promotion.

Gut instincts are simply subconscious suggestions that arise from all of the patterns we have observed. In other words, your gut instinct tells you more than you can logically know, because it represents much, much more information than you could ever logically process.

BUT WHAT HAPPENS WHEN YOUR GUT IS WRONG?

The bottom line is that you should trust your instincts. That being said, how do you explain the fact that sometimes our gut instincts are wrong? Executives that Hayashi interviewed were quick to admit that their instincts have often been wrong. According to Hayashi, there are a couple of factors that prevent us from realizing how faulty our intuition can be. The first is a tendency toward revisionism. And the second is our tendency toward overconfidence. Hayashi says various surveys have found that we overestimate our ability in just about everything we do.

I think what happens is this: Your subconscious mind has been improperly programmed because of one of two things: either because the data (patterns) going in are false or the conclusions that you keep attaching to them are invalid.

For example, let's say that every Thursday you put on a blue wool suit and discovered that when you put your hand on your office door you get a shock. The pattern you've been noticing is valid. Blue suit. Thursday. Shock. But if you concluded that the problem was Thursday or the color blue, you'd be wrong.

A different example: You read in the newspaper that violent crime keeps rising. You read story after story of terrible things happening on the street. You conclude that it's safer to stay inside. Then you find out that all those stories were fabrications. Your decision about your safety was valid but the data was wrong.

This type of bad programming is common for two reasons. First, we all have a capacity to misinterpret our own experiences. Second, we can easily fall victim to indirect "faulty" experiences from things we read and see on television. These secondary experiences can "feel" very real to the subconscious mind. They can be internalized just as readily, I believe, as primary experiences.

For example, as a marketing guy, I know this: If I want to sell you an insurance product, I have to stir up your uncertainties, even your fears. I can do that by creating little stories that make the point I want to make. So if I want to sell you accident insurance, for example, I'll write 10 terrible tales about accident victims. By the time you've read three of them, you will have an internal, subconscious pattern in favor of accident insurance established.

When I teach copywriting at American Writers & Artists Institute (AWAI) seminars, I train writers to do just that. By showing rather than telling, I teach them to create in their prospect a deep experience—one that involves feelings, thoughts, and desires—that will serve the selling objective.

Also, there is the problem of perspective. Take any experience— a ball game, a traffic accident, or a business meeting— and ask four people what took place. Chances are you'll get four different answers. That's because the answers are based on each person's perspective and past history, so therefore different elements of the same experience may or may not stand out. This means that the event's pattern that is subconsciously recorded will be different for different people. And some of those patterns will simply be wrong.

SO HOW DO YOU EDUCATE YOUR GUT INSTINCT?

How do you develop a powerful business intuition that is much, much better than that of the average leader?

First, you've got to be very careful about the patterns you internalize, because they will determine your gut instinct later on. For example, we all know that a woman in an old Victorian house should not go into the basement alone. Yet, none of us has been hacked to death for doing so. We all know that the ozone layer is disappearing and that the oceans are rising. Yet, we've never actually seen an ozone layer or measured the ocean tide.

Most importantly, trust more in your experience than in the experience of others. When it comes to business, learn from what has actually happened to you, not from what has supposedly happened to others. A good leader will make every effort to pay close and objective attention to his primary experiences. And he'll be very skeptical of everything he reads or hears about, however enticing. Remember, the experience of others may be distorted by misperception or miscommunication. Your experience, if you are lucid, is genuine.

Trusting in your experience doesn't mean trusting the conclusions you draw. As explained above, we are all prone to incorrect inductions. Challenge your conclusions and interpretations by talking to others. After an important incident, one that might have suggested a lesson to you, have a conversation with others. How did they see what happened? What lessons did the draw? You should still give primary weight to your own reactions, but temper them by listening to the interpretations of others. Analyze every business deal you do. Ask yourself:

- What went right?
- What went wrong?
- How could it have been better?
- How could it have been worse?

Again, ask your colleagues for their opinions. Do they agree with your views on what went right and wrong? If not, why? Resist the impulse to make yourself "right" in retrospect. The conclusions you draw from your actual primary business experiences are the most valuable resources you have. They are the foundation of your future decisions, the bedrock on which your future success will be built.

Make sure those conclusions are valid and your instinct for making the right decisions, in any situation, will inevitably get better. Eventually you'll be seen as a great leader with a born gift, but only you and I will know your great intuition was a skill you worked hard to develop.

A few years ago I read an article in Industry Week by the chairman of Penton Media, Sal Marino. He talked about a book that changed the way he viewed gut instinct decisions. It's called Decision Traps[17] by Professors' J. Edward Russo and Paul J.H. Shoemaker. After reading the book, Marino said he spent more time finding factual information about issues instead of deciding by his gut, and his decision making "batting average" improved. In the book the professors list 10 reasons why most people make mistakes when making gut decisions. I think they're relevant and will help you hone your gut instinct. They are:

1. Plunging in. Reaching conclusions before taking the time to think about all of the issues.
2. Frame blindness. Failing to recognize the real issue and working on the wrong one.
3. Lack of control. Only defining an issue in one way and not looking at the alternatives.
4. Overconfidence in judgment. Being too sure of your own opinions and not gathering important factual information.
5. Shortsighted shortcuts—Using only "rules of thumb" and convenient facts.
6. Shooting from the hip—"Winging it" instead of following a systematic decision making process.
7. Group failure—Falsely assuming that because so many good people are part of the process, good choices will result. This happens often when the leader doesn't manage the decision-making process.
8. Fooling ourselves—Forgetting to examine the results of past outcomes. Often times this happens because we're protecting our egos or fall victim to hindsight.
9. Not keeping track—Failing to analyze results and examine lessons that are available.
10. Failing to audit the process—Not creating an organized approach to the decision making process. (See chapter 6 for a simple and effective decision making process you should use every time you've something important to decide!)

---

17 Marino, Sal "Rely on science, not your gut." *Industry Week*, Jan 24, 2000 quoting Russo, J. Edward, Shoemaker, Paul J.H., *Decision Traps*, Doubleday: 1989.

[KEY POINT]

The best leaders are not highly competitive. Instead they share their secrets and help others. Leaders understand that vital business secrets in almost any area don't need to be coveted because they can't be copied exactly. And when it comes to internal competition, leaders strive to eliminate it entirely by creating common goals.

CHAPTER 8:
ARE YOU TOO COMPETITIVE?

"Man has risen so far above all other species that he competes in ways unique in nature. He fights by means of complicated weapons; he fights for ends remote in time."
~Charles A. Lindbergh, *Autobiography of Values*, 1978[18]

Hollywood would have you believe that successful businessmen are competitive creatures who fight their way to the top. And there are plenty of best–selling business books that support that view. I've done some competing in my own career and have seen some brutal things done in the pursuit of leadership.

But I don't believe that all that nasty behavior is good business. In fact, I think it's counter productive. Yes, horrible people sometimes succeed in business, but it's not their meanness and greed that works for them. It's some positive quality—usually hard work and tenacity— that is propelling them forward, not the scheming and cheating they believe in.

Let me explain by putting forward several postulates. Bad behav-

---

18 Lindbergh, Charles A. *Autobiography of Values*, 1978, Harvest Books: Reprint 1992

ior limits your potential because it stems from a view that one's talents are limited. If you believe that the only way you can succeed is by cheating or lying, for example, you'll be inclined to cheat and lie every time you think about succeeding.

In and of itself this kind of behavior is self-destructive, but when you're a leader it's even more damaging— harming your goals, your business, and your reputation. In an article in *The Chief Executive*, Robert Bunker CEO of Aperture, a physician credentialing company says "Leadership has never been rocket science. It's just a matter of being honest and true, having integrity."[19]

While I think leadership is quite a bit more than that, integrity does play an important role. I believe a leader must set an example of what is acceptable behavior to achieve success within an organization. In my experience, choosing to ignore a selfish, inward-looking, competitive philosophy is part of setting a good example. Basically, I've learned that the golden rule of "do unto others" holds true in business too. Good behavior will open new doors for you. Although it may not be apparent on a case-by-case basis, altruistic efforts produce very profound, long-term returns. The good things you do in business, good actions whose purposes are directed outside yourself, repay you in countless ways—some financial, some social, some personal.

Competition in and of itself can be good or bad depending on the intention.

When competition is good its purpose is play and there is no desire associated with winning. When it's bad its goal is diminishing the opponent and there is anguish in losing. In business, there is such thing as healthy competition when it comes to your direct competitors. But by that I mean using their presence to inspire you and your business to perform better.

And the good leaders in my opinion don't take it any further. If you think it's necessary to dupe and deceive your way to the top you'll never enjoy the satisfaction you seek, regardless of what trophies you pick up along the way.

Learn to succeed by sharing and helping and innovating and thinking, and you'll have a long and happy career.

---

19 Robert Bunker, Quoted in *"Saving Your Skin: CEO 2 CEO Discussion"*, The Chief Executive, Jan. 2002.

SHARING WHAT YOU KNOW IS KEY— EVEN YOUR SECRETS.

I can tell you from personal experience that in the jewelry business, the art business, the contest and sweepstakes business, the astrology business, the academic-book-publishing business, and many others—sharing ideas with your competitors works much better than trying to take advantage of them to further your own ends.

Let me explain. I recently returned from a day-long "roundtable" of top executives in the financial publishing industry. Twenty-four executives, representing many of the most successful businesses in the market, sat around a table in a small London hotel and told one another some of their best secrets.

Why did we do it? Because most of us are old enough to realize four important things:

1. Most of the vital business secrets in marketing, sales, motivation, management, and so on, don't need to be coveted because they can't be copied exactly. In every business, they need to be reinvented to fit and then executed. In doing so, they become distinct.
2. Usually, you will do better if your competitors do well. Success creates success. Markets expand when good ideas are adapted by all. Great marketing ideas are meant to be copied. They create more demand, increase the market, and provide dividends for everyone.
3. Most of your best secrets will never be copied anyway, even if you beg your peers to copy them. That's because only you really understand how powerful they are. And even when your colleague does "get it," he'll have a hellish time getting the people in his business to understand it, let alone implement it.
4. An exchange of ideas ultimately benefits everyone.

THE PROBLEM WITH INTERNAL COMPETITION

Just as it's not good to let competition drive your external business

---

20 Covey, Steven R. *7 Habits of Highly Effective People*, Simon & Schuster; 1st edition: September 15, 1990.

DO YOU HAVE A "COMPETITIVE PROBLEM"?

Start thinking about your own competitive instincts. Are you too competitive? You can get a good idea of where you stand by answering the following questions:

1. Are you motivated primarily by the desire to do better than someone else?
2. Are you suspicious of your competitors?
3. Are you suspicious of your colleagues?
4. Do you secretly enjoy it when a competitor fails?
5. Do you like to see your peers fail too?

If you answered "yes" more than once, you are probably overly competitive. I know it doesn't feel that way. You see yourself as "realistic." You suspect that I am naïve.

If you answered "no" to all five questions, you don't have a "competitive problem." But that doesn't mean you're destined to succeed. You still need to work hard and engage in all the get-ahead behaviors. But at least you won't waste any time and energy trying to slow other people down when you should be pushing forward with your plan.

decisions, it's also not good to let competition run rampant *within* your business. Steven R. Covey (the "Seven Habits" guy)[20] astutely points out that some entrepreneurs make the mistake of trying to get their people to compete inside the company. "They think this will enhance productivity," he says, "but what it really does is create conflicts and interdepartmental rivalry."

He's absolutely right about that. I know. I have done it both ways. My earliest instinct was to set good people against one another, hoping it would drive them to achieve more. Instead, what I got was a lot of negative, unproductive behaviors. For example, managers were withholding vital information from one another, taking potshots at each other, and spending a lot of energy beating people down instead of making better products and selling them more effectively.

If you're already in an internally competitive environment, all's not lost. There are ways to diffuse the situation. One of the best is to create common goals. According to Kathleen Eisenhardt's 10-year research of management in more than 12 entrepreneurial firms, the most accomplished created a shared vision through common goals. These are "goals that stress collective success or common enemies." Their sole purpose is to make everyone feel like they're on the same team. A second way to ease internal competition according to Eisenhardt, is to define "clear areas of responsibility."[21] I agree. As the leader you should lead, but that doesn't mean micromanaging your employees. If you micromanage you'll not only waste your time, you'll rob your employees of valuable experiences that will help them grow and help your business grow.

21 Eisenhardt, Kathleen M. 'Strategy as Strategic Decision-Making" *Sloan Management Review*, Spring, 1999.

CHAPTER 9:
MIND YOUR MANNERS

"Rudeness is the weak man's imitation of strength."
—Eric Hoffer, *The Passionate State of Mind*, 1954[22]

Winning friends is a good way of creating a supportive network, but it's not the best way to influence your employees. The best leaders I know don't concern themselves with being liked. Their focus is squarely on the business. But that being said; arrogance and rudeness is unnecessary and truly counterproductive. If your employees actively dislike you, you'll have a hard time getting them to follow your lead.

If you want to reach all of your business goals with the least interference you must learn to be instinctively considerate. How do you do that? It's very simple—you practice good manners.

GOOD MANNERS 101

Being well-mannered means acknowledging people each time you meet them, remembering their names and something about them,

---

22   Hoffer, Eric *The Passionate State of Mind*, 1954, Buccaneer Books: Reprint, August 1998.

expressing yourself in a thoughtful manner, and saying "please" and "thank you" every time it's called for. If you are well mannered you are usually also:

- well dressed
- well groomed
- well spoken

Having good manners also means that you DON"T:

- interrupt meetings
- break into conversations
- send angry emails
- speak badly about fellow workers
- pass rumors
- shout
- use vulgarities in speech
- embarrass your employees
- criticize in public

You might be thinking that you'd never be rude to your coworkers or subordinates. But it's surprisingly simple to forget your manners as you climb the ladder of success. With each step up in power and prestige, it's that much easier to ignore a courtesy or to take one without thanks. Eventually, if you don't watch yourself, you can turn into a character you wouldn't like if you saw him on television or in the movies.

I've mentioned some of the things you shouldn't do above. Here are ten things you *should* do if you want to be thought of as polite and considerate.

HOW TO BE WELL-MANNERED IN BUSINESS

1. Smile and say "hello" to everyone you meet each day. (Including your assistant.)
2. Listen attentively when your subordinates speak, even if what

they are saying makes little or no sense.

3. Always speak with a positive tone of voice.
4. Say "thank you" every time it's warranted.
5. In casual conversation, show concern for the other person. Ask questions. Don't just answer them.
6. Praise people specifically and publicly.
7. When you do something that hurts someone's feelings, apologize quickly.
8. When you make a mistake admit it immediately and set it right.
9. Bring solutions with your problems.
10. Know and use the first and last names of all of those who report to you.

MANNERS FOR BUSINESS EVENTS

Good manners are even more critical when you are attending a business dinner or some other business-related social function. These events give you the opportunity to either improve or degrade the opinion others have of you. Only a foolish person would ignore this fact. It all boils down to this: You are at that business dinner to further your business interests. Treat it with the same seriousness as you do your business. Here are 9 rules to remember at your next professional soiree:

1. Do not drink too much. It doesn't make you nearly as likeable as you think it does.
2. Don't talk too much about yourself. Spend most of your time asking questions of and listening to others—especially those you want to impress.
3. Be positive.
4. When introducing people, always say something complimentary about them.
5. When seating yourself and your date at a large table, be sure to observe the boy-girl seating tradition. That means seating your partner next to someone of the opposite sex. If you fail to do so, you cause a bit of a problem not only for the people you are

next to but also for another couple that will come later.

6. Don't look as if you are in pain, even if you are.
7. Don't discuss politics or religion.
8. Don't talk about your problems.
9. Address each person at the table at least once during the meal.

SAY "THANK YOU" IN WRITING

If someone does you a favor send them a short, hand-written thank you note on professional looking stationary to mark your appreciation. All it takes is a few minutes to jot down a sincere word of thanks but the rewards for your small effort will be big. Not only will you be seen as a well-mannered professional, a note can help you forge or maintain a very useful business relationship.

If you've no time for a note, make a phone call, or send a quick email to express your gratitude. For the highly organized, you can have email "thank you note" templates prepared and simply fill in the personal information of recipient. This takes no time at all and you'll still get credit for your effort!

E-MAIL ETIQUETTE

Speaking of email, I recently witnessed a messy situation when a memo, sent in confidence, was either inadvertently or purposely routed back to the "wrong" person. What resulted was a mix of bad feelings, confusion, and a derailed relationship that will take some mending. The damage caused goes beyond the two people directly involved.

What is especially unfortunate is that the wording of the memo was almost certainly an exaggeration. It didn't represent the truth, though it was taken as such. We sometimes exaggerate for impact, but usually when it is "safe." So what is safe and what isn't in an e-mail?

I think it's best to look at this way. If you write something negative about someone, there is a better than 50% chance that it will find its way to him. Since the statement is written, it can't be denied, it can't be erased and it is harder to explain away. Most likely, it will even seem harsher than it was meant to be in the eyes of the "victim." This means real trouble for you.

When it comes to email etiquette, I like to follow this general principle. Praise in public, criticize in private.

Write your memos as if they were public announcements. Never write anything about someone that you wouldn't say to him personally. Actually, the test is should be more severe than that—especially if you're angry: Never write anything about someone that you wouldn't say to him in public!

Needless to say, such an approach will have a "chilling effect" on frankness. That is a price to pay, but it is not, in my view, too heavy a price. It means you must be careful about your criticisms, that you must not exaggerate them, that you must put them in context, that you must make them specific, and that you can't be sarcastic or snide.

If you practice this careful public criticism, you will get good at it and it won't seem as restrictive as it does now. It will make you a better, more precise and fairer critic. And that's not so terrible. Yes, you'll work harder. Yes, you'll have to think longer before you write. But you'll feel wiser, more powerful, and in control.

But the battle isn't over even after you've learned to control what YOU say. You have to be vigilant to keep your correspondents' comments confidential.

Promise yourself this: Starting today, you will assume that anything you write about anybody will eventually be read by him or her. So frame your comments accordingly. If at all possible, say what needs to be said directly to that person. If you can't, do it via a personal phone call (making sure you are not being taped or broadcast—you laugh but it happens!) And to avoid spreading slander, make it a habit to double-check the "recipient" box before you forward or copy any e-mail message!

TELEPHONE ETIQUETTE

In the world of email, businesses are relying less and less on the phone to communicate. But that doesn't mean you can let your telephone skills slip.

Remember basic courtesies. For example, before you put someone on hold, let him know approximately how long he will be left waiting. ("May I put you on hold for about three to four minutes while I talk to Mr. Jones about this?") Be sure to get back to him before the requested time, even if it is only to tell him you need more time. Make the effort to do this, and you'll return to a happier caller.

Leave clear phone messages. If you don't, not only will you risk the recipient being confused about what course of action to take, but you won't have made a very strong impression. Here are four things you should always do when you leave a message:

1. Leave your name.
2. Keep your message short—one sentence is best.
3. Establish a time frame for call-back.
4. Repeat your contact information at least twice.

If, like me, you are much happier in the world of email and don't like talking on the phone, try an idea suggested in a book by Paul LeBon entitled *Escape from Voicemail Hell*.[23] In the book, LeBon suggests that when you want to send a colleague a personal message—a thank you, congratulations, or birthday wishes—call him at his office late at night when he's sure to miss your call but will pick it up first thing in the morning. You'll get credit for the call without the dreaded conversation, and he gets your message in the personal way you meant to send it.

Manners are not a fundamental part of leadership. To become a distinguished leader you don't need to smile and be friendly. Instead, it is strong business skills and the ability to articulate a vision that will set you apart from your peers. But courtesy, consideration and good manners *will* make your journey as a leader much smoother. And everything you want to accomplish will get done more quickly and easily.

---

23 LeBon, Paul, Karam, Sara, *Escape From Voicemail Hell / Boost Your Productivity By Making Voicemail Work For You*, ParLeau Publishing, October, 1999.

PART TWO

LEAD BY EXAMPLE: SECRETS OF THE MOVERS AND SHAKERS

CHAPTER 10
#1: COMING UP WITH THE BIG IDEA

"The real true source of power in any company today is ideas—the rest is housekeeping."
~Marsh Fisher, Co, Founder of Century 21 Real Estate

As a leader your primary role is to figure out what your organization should be doing not just now but in the future. Imagining what can be usually calls for a big idea, a notion of how things can be better, cheaper, faster, easier—something that will propel your business to the next level.

This is not an easy task. Your idea must be big enough to inspire followers, useful enough to create benefits (for your customers, your employees and yourself) and cost effective.

And ultimately it must be right. There is nothing so dispiriting and financially damaging than a big idea that changes systems, drains resources, taxes everyone's patience and then falls flat on its face, a financially disastrous failure.

With all those requirements it's no wonder that very few people are even willing to step forward with big, new ideas. Criticizing existing operations—that's common. But being willing to stand up before the rest of the company and make an argument for change—that takes guts.

HAVE COURAGE

So let's call that the first requirement of the process. To be able to come up with big, new ideas you have to have the courage to be wrong. Wise men don't drum up their courage foolishly. They derive it from thinking, planning and testing.

THINK WELL

An effective leader thinks efficiently. He does not fret away his time worrying about the minor problems of the business nor does he concern himself with problems other people can solve. If you want to become (or maintain yourself as) the big idea man in your company you should focus your thinking to the two or three areas that are critical to your business.

For most businesses these areas are:

- Generating efficient new sales to produce growth
- Creating vertical, back end sales to boos profits
- Improving product quality to ensure customer retention

Each of these areas demands different approaches. To come up with new selling ideas you have to become a student of your own selling strategies and the selling strategies of your competitors.

When I consult with an office furniture business, for example, I make it a policy to know every advertising campaign they have done in recent years, how it performed, what kind of customers it brought in, how much they spent, how much they refunded, etc. Once I've mastered that information I try to do the same thing with their primary competitors. Somewhere along the line I begin to see how the business really works. I see the invisible links that hold each selling operation together and begin to understand the fundamental psychology that supports all of the most successful advertising campaigns. As I master this information, ideas begin to come to me. I wonder if A company used the pricing strategy of B Company but with the copy approach of D company. What would happen then?

DON'T GET DISCOURAGED

I don't expect to come up with great ideas in the beginning. But after immersing myself in the materials of selling ideas do come. By asking questions about the ideas that come I can quickly determine whether they've been tried before and if so, with what kind of quality and with what results.

If my initial ideas don't amount to much, I don't get discouraged. I know that if I keep studying the sales efforts of competitors and compare them to my clients sooner or later some useful new idea will come to me.

KNOW YOUR INDUSTRY INSIDE AND OUT

I use a somewhat different approach to thinking about coming up with back end products. Here I focus on the initial advertising campaign. I study it closely to try to understand what exactly the customers were responding to. Were they interested in office furniture that allowed them to work more productively? Or did they want to project a certain image with their furniture—powerful, professional, or creative?

Once I've discovered the secret foundation of my client's initial sale I have a psychological basis on which to create many back end products. I begin with the premise that what a customer bought once he'll

---

5-POINT CHECKLIST: HOW TO EVALUATE A BIG IDEA

Whether it's your big idea or someone else's, there are five very simple questions you can ask that will help you quickly determine its strengths and weaknesses:

1. Whom does it benefit?
2. How great are the benefits?
3. Does it take advantage of the company's market advantage?
4. Will the benefits outweigh the costs?
5. What do we do if it doesn't work?

buy a second time. And what he bought a second time he'll buy again.

I create products that are thus the same as the lead generating product in their basic psychological appeal, but different in respect to other factors:

- Pricing
- Packaging
- Size, quantity, frequency, etc.

The same basic psychological benefit—let's say a book that promises to make you feel better about yourself—can be repackaged in many different ways:

- A $79 audio cassette program
- A series of $15 books
- A $599 home study program
- A $1950 two-day seminar

Get to know the industry and you'll get to know the many ways you can package a product. By constructing a grid of boxes—different prices along one axis and different product packaging formats along the other—you can often come up with a dozen or more good back—end product ideas in a single sitting.

ASK QUESTIONS

Coming up with good ideas for improving the product is relatively easy. All you need to do is ask. Ask your customers by phoning them, writing them, emailing them and surveying them.

Keep in mind that sometimes they will give you answers that they think are "good answers" rather than truthful answers. Read between the lines. But if you ask them they will tell you.

Ask your customer service people. They understand customer reaction in group terms. They understand the major gripes, the nagging issues and the trends.

Don't rely on the views of a single customer service person because he may be biased. Ask as many as you can.

Ask the people who make the product, especially the people on the manufacturing line.

Ask them, "What are the three best things about this product" and also "What are the three worst things about this product?" What they tell you might astonish you.

By doing your homework in these three critical areas— front—end sales, back—end development and product improvement—you will have a constant stream of good ideas popping into your head.

TALK TO A COLLEAGUE

Discuss these ideas with trusted colleagues and as soon as you have the wrinkles ironed out, bring them up at meetings.

PLAN YOUR PRESENTATION

Don't just shoot from the hip. Plan your comments carefully. Memorize the first and last sentence of your presentation, however casual it may appear.

Make sure you have impressive and persuasive data to support your claims.

Explain very clearly how the customer will benefit from the idea first and then explain how everyone else will too. Summarize your main points succinctly.

PREPARE FOR REJECTION

Be prepared to have your big ideas rejected when you first suggest them. Almost every one of the big ideas I've come up with has been roundly denigrated when I first suggested them.

But if you can be open to criticism and flexible enough to make sensible modifications your big ideas will get better and better as time goes by and your critics will eventually become your supporters.

KEEP THOROUGH RECORDS

One last thing—document in writing your suggestions and keep a record of them so that when your big idea changes the company's future and everyone else is trying to take credit for it, you'll have proof it was your idea.

Strong leaders don't wait for a consensus to push through their ideas—ideas both big and small. Instead, these leaders put their energy into garnering support from the top, from only a few powerful people. Then they work their way down.

#2: DON'T WAIT FOR CONSENSUS

"To do great things is difficult; but to command great things is more difficult."
~Friedrich Nietzsche, Thus Spake Zarathustra, 1883-92

In the past few years I've read a lot about leadership and consensus building. The business experts who write these articles assert that the most effective way to accomplish a goal is to spend a good deal of time in the beginning promoting the idea to the rank and file. If you fail to do that the argument goes, your idea will not succeed because it won't get the grass roots support it needs to flourish. If you do create a consensus before you make any moves, then your idea will be accomplished with acceptance and understanding. This line of reasoning makes a lot of sense to me. Getting your goal accomplished is bound to be easier if you have less resistance.

But when I think about my own experience in leadership, I can't say that I was a great consensus builder. And when I think about the successful business leaders I know—the men and women who have rallied large groups of people to accomplish important things—not a single one of them would I categorize as a consensus builder.

So what's going on? Maybe all my friends and I are not true leaders but simply bullies and bosses who manage to accomplish their goals without consensus by badgering, belittling, threatening and so on. Maybe, but again I don't feel like that is true. If not that, then what?

CONSENSUS BUILDING: THE BIG MISTAKE

Maybe those who advocate consensus building are simply wrong. Maybe consensus building, while it seems very sensible, is actually a mistake. A recent Harvard Business Review story suggests as much. Great leaders, the article says, have one thing in common: a burning desire to accomplish their goals as soon as possible. Although the men and women studied admitted to being "in favor of" consensus building, an examination of their actual day-to-day business management practices indicates that they didn't actually do much of it.

Here's a good example from my own business life: Several weeks ago I woke up with the idea that my major client should change the way it views itself and projects itself in public. Previously it saw itself as a marketing company. In the future, I argued, you should think of yourself as product makers. Needless to say, this would be a major transformation affecting almost everyone in the business and all the hundreds of thousands of customers. It is a metamorphosis that would cost the business time and money and would involve the enthusiastic cooperation of hundreds of people.

BUILDING SUPPORT THE RIGHT WAY

Here's what I'm doing to promote it: First I wrote a letter to three people, the Chairman, the CEO and a trusted advisor. The Chairman was my target. It was really his decision that was required to get it going. But I knew that if the CEO opposed it wouldn't go anywhere, even if the Chairman and I were in favor of it.

I included the trusted advisor because I suspected he would like my suggestion and I was hoping he would influence the Chairman to agree. So far, I haven't spoken to anyone else in the business about this. I know it would be dangerous to do so before the Chairman got on board. So instead of stirring up the troops with a grass roots campaign I'm focusing on getting only two people to buy in—the chairman and the CEO. If you call that consensus building, then I am in favor of it.

After I get the green light from them, I will attempt to "convert" three of the eight regional vice presidents to my idea. I will do so with a series of group emails and personal phone calls. I will also propose the idea to the other regional VPs, but I won't spend any individual attention on them.

When I get my three VPs to back my plan, then I will push to have the goal formalized. From that point forward I won't treat the subject as if it's up for discussion. I will treat it as a fait accompli. The reason? I don't want to undermine its potential by building on the murky soil of debate. I'd prefer to spend my energy on getting the grumblers to understand or forcing them to shut up.

In this company of 500 people, in other words, I am looking to get only 5 or 6 individuals to buy into my idea. That cannot be said to be consensus building, but I know it is the most effective way of making the transformation completely and quickly.

YOU NEED ONLY THE SUPPORT OF KEY PEOPLE

I believe my strategy in this instance is typical of most successful leaders. We want to achieve our goals completely, correctly and quickly. We see the goal as something good for everyone—whether they understand it or not. We know that if we can get certain key people to support us the rank and file will follow. We know this is true because we've seen it take place in the past and because we understand the nature of most workers—they don't want to resist. They want to make their days as easy and enjoyable as possible.

We also understand that there may be a few influential leaders who will oppose us. But if we isolate them by surrounding them with equally strong leaders who agree with us, we can push the project forward and work on getting them to cooperate properly later. In other words, successful leaders achieve their goals by selling them to a select group of influential people. They do so for three reasons:

1. They are very excited about a project when they embrace it.
2. They visualize it in its completed state and imagine all the benefits it will bring. This gives them a sense of enthusiasm—and a very strong desire to accomplish it.
3. Although they believe in their goal, they are never 100% sure

it will work. In an ordinary person this might create the desire to wait and think it out some more. In the successful leader it creates the desire to get going with it as fast as possible because the successful person knows that you will never know whether an idea makes sense unless you try it. The sooner I can get people to do this, the successful leader thinks, the sooner I'll know whether it is a good idea.

DON'T BELIEVE IN COMMON JUDGMENT

Successful leaders don't believe in the value of a common judgment. They don't think that a good idea can be discovered by a public discussion or debate. They have found that in the past such experiences led to either an idea so watered down that it didn't have any force or a goal so challenged that it had no chance of being accepted.

FOLLOW THE LEAD OF THE GREAT LEADERS

To get your good ideas accomplished follow the lead of the great leaders before you: don't look for consensus. In fact don't even talk about your idea except to a few influential people. Sell them until they are completely sold. If it takes longer than you expected, so be it. You won't succeed without your core group. So sell them hard.

Once that is done announce the idea to the management group as a fait accompli, but ask for suggestions. If and when a sensible objection is raised, figure out what to do about it but don't give up on your goal unless you really lose faith in it. Don't give up because you want a consensus.

Once your goal has been modified to make it stronger (and it should be modified for no other reason) then take it to the troops. At that point you should expect everyone to execute it well and faithfully—even the managers who may have been opposed to it at first.

$$\left[\text{ KEY POINT }\right]$$

Ideas are central to strong leadership and so is the ability to test them. Good leaders use a 6-step plan to ensure their best ideas make it from concept stage to testing. They also know how to overcome doubts and objections to keep the momentum going. If their idea succeeds, they push on; and if it fails, they move on to the next idea.

#3: STRENGTHEN YOUR IDEAS: THE LEAP FROM CONTEMPLATION TO TESTING

"A rock pile ceases to be a rock pile the moment a single man contemplates it, bearing within him the image of a cathedral."
~Antoine-Marie-Roger de Saint-Exupery (1900-1944)

As we've discussed in earlier chapters, the first secret to good leadership is being able to cultivate new ideas. Some executives are full of new ideas. And if there's one quality that you need to keep a good organization working it's new ideas. These good leaders take the time to think about how to make things better in every way, and they generate ideas to that effect. But be careful not to spend too much time thinking. Take only the time that is necessary to think through a new idea to make sure it really works. After that, the validity of any goal or objective can't be determined by thought or debate; it can only be found by putting the idea to the test—by doing it. New ideas must get results: they must be good for business. They must increase production or improve quality or reduce refunds or raise profits.

The difference between an ordinary idea man that doesn't get much done and an individual who is able to take charge and launch his business to new levels of achievement is often a simple thing: the willingness to put those ideas into play, to test them out to see if they are as good as they seem. This is the mark of a true leader.

I sympathize with those who would just as soon keep leave their best ideas in the board room. Clever thoughts make for inspiring conversations and inspiring conversations can often bring you acknowledgement—yet without risk. Insisting that your good idea get tried out on the shop floor—that's a bold thing to do and requires either a great deal of confidence or a staunch heart (usually both.)

FIGHT TO TEST YOUR BEST IDEAS

The most effective leaders I know tend to push hard to get their ideas done. In some cases they do so with skill and ease. In other cases they simply push. At all times their focus is on finding out if the idea "really works." If it doesn't they are not happy, but they usually don't wile away their time feeling sorry for themselves. After a brief period of questioning (and maybe cursing and moaning), the wake up with a new idea and begin the pushing process all over again.

I'm a perfect example. Once I have a new idea in my head I can't let it go. I'm involved in this process right now trying to convince one of my clients to make a major change in his business. I suggested the idea about two weeks ago in response to a problem we (the Chairman, CEO, and I) were talking about. Since then I've written at least a dozen follow up memos of increasing urgency. Some explain in different words, or in more detail, my basic idea. Some refute "problems" and "concerns" the Chairman and CEO voiced. My feeling is, "This idea can make a dramatic improvement in the business. I'm not positive its right but the reward is so great why don't we test it?"

It's not so much that I want the gratification of seeing my idea acted out it's more that I'd like to discover—after arguing about if for two weeks—whether I'm right. Since I'm so eager to find out if my idea will work (and if it doesn't, get on with the next thing), and since I don't believe I'll know if it will work until I put it to the test, the only path that makes sense to me is to do everything I can to execute it as soon as possible.

JUMPSTART YOUR IDEA TESTING

What about those projects that you can't seem to get out of the idea phase? Maybe there's a project you've been trying to test for a long while. You've already got key people involved, and you've been patient, but nothing has happened. What do you do? One of the most common reasons for failure is the unwillingness to move beyond obstacles. I don't know whether it's caused by laziness, fear (or both), but it's something you should recognize and deal with when you see it affecting your projects. There's one course of action you can take to get results, simply follow these 3 tests:

Ask the people involved for a specific list of all the doubts and objections they have about your idea/project.

Make a list of suggestions as to how to overcome these doubts and objections. Make this list available to an outside team of qualified people. Make everyone involved understand the importance of momentum. The sooner you can get the idea moving, the faster you can fix the problems. Explain clearly that until the new idea is actually out in the market for a field test, all the problems and objections imagined are simply that—imaginary.

My idea per se doesn't make me a leader in this case. It's the combination of having a new idea and my willingness to push and pull—to do whatever it takes—to get it tested.

I don't want my idea to be implemented if it's going to hurt the business. I'm not driven by that kind of ego-need. I realize that anything that is not truly helpful will eventually be hurtful—and not just to the company but to me personally. So that's why I'm happy to test it out.

6 STEPS TO TESTING YOUR IDEA

If you are full of good ideas but haven't had a great deal of success in having them tested, consider the READY-FIRE-AIM strategy:

1. Write your new idea down. Sleep on it for a day, a week or a month. (Get ready!)
2. Relate it to someone whose opinion you trust and discuss it until the idea has been whipped into shape.
3. Try the idea out on one or several more people, preferably influential people who will participate in its execution. Again, make whatever improvements seem logical.
4. Backed by a strengthened idea and the support of several key people, use all the muscle you can muster to get the project done quickly and properly and then put it to a reliable test in the marketplace. (Fire!)
5. If the market responds well to your idea, the next step is to refine it in degrees to increase its potential for success. (Aim Higher!)
6. If the idea doesn't work in the test stage, don't waste your time. Scrap it and move on to the next idea…

DON'T BE AFRAID TO FAIL

Just because an idea failed doesn't mean you did. Mahatma Gandhi once said "full effort is full victory." Always remember that some of your ideas—maybe many of them—will *fail*. But taking that chance is the only way you'll find out if an idea is good, and remember, all it takes to succeed is a few good ideas—and some have done it on less!

Good leaders spend time strengthening and focusing their ideas. But they also make preparations for selling their plan to their employees. They set easy to communicate and easy to understand goals. Then they follow a 6 step strategy to convince their employees the idea is a good one and will result in many benefits.

#4: SETTING A GOAL AND RALLYING THE TROOPS

"In the province of the mind, what one believes to be true either is true or becomes so."
~John Lilly

You have an idea about how your business can do something new or better. You have run that idea through a gauntlet of trusted colleagues, individuals with the intelligence, and experience to pummel the air hot air out of it.

The result is something stronger, more focused, and more powerful than the original—something that has a good chance of achieving the benefits (increased sales, decreased refunds, etc.) that you imagined in the first place.

Plus, it now has the support of several of the company's key leaders—the very people who initially beat it up for you.

You are excited to get it going—and the sooner, the better.

Your impulse is to gather the troops and make a public announcement or to send out a bulk e-mail letting everyone know how their world is going to change.

But you shouldn't do so. Not just yet.

FIRST, SET YOUR GOALS

There is one more step you must take before the big leap. You must convert your good, trim, tested idea into a goal—or, more likely, a set of specific goals that have two qualities:

1. They are easy to understand.
2. They are easy to implement.

You will achieve the first goal by carefully crafting a short (less than one page is preferable) memo that explains the goal in simple terms, using specific examples and easy-to-grasp analogies, if needed.

You can make your goal easy to implement by breaking it into a series of smaller tasks. What you are aiming for is a step-by-step map that gets your management (those who will be responsible for making your idea happen) from where you are today to exactly where you want to be, based on your carefully articulated goal memo.

PREPARING YOUR STRATEGY TO RALLY THE TROOPS

When you've done all that, you are ready to rally the rank and file. This is fundamentally a selling process.

You are selling an idea to a group of people who may not know you very well. To be an effective leader you must not only discover useful ideas and persuade your key people to follow them, but also get everyone else in the organization excited about and open to your project.

The primary way you do that is through your key people. Assign each of them the task of persuading their own staff.

But supply them with the all the persuasive tools they will need. Selling the troops on your idea is a harder job than selling your key people. The rank and file is less committed to your satisfaction, further removed from your good intentions, less experienced in strategic thinking and—frankly—not sure they should give a scrap for what you want. You have to do your homework if you're going to succeed.

The basic 6-step strategy I use is this:

1. Make a Promise—what is the largest single benefit that your idea or project offers the business. This is the big promise you will sell the troops on.

2. Create a Picture—how will this benefit make the lives of your employees and the lives of your customers better and/or easier? Create several statements that will allow your troops to visualize themselves in this better place.

3. Explain the Benefits—explain using specific instances of how your employees and customers will be better off because of your idea or project.

4. Make Claims and Prove Them—back those specific instances from above up with proof. If "a" happens then "b" happens

5. Anticipate and Answer Objections— you must understand the fears before they are articulated, anticipate problems before they occur, and have answers ready before they are asked. The best way to do all that is to sit down for a private few hours and draw up a list of every possible misunderstanding, concern, or negative ramification your idea might create. Write them down on one side of a sheet of paper—and on the opposite side, write down answers.

6. Provide Assurances—make sure all of your answers are good ones. When there are no good answers, but you still strongly believe in the idea, find a way to say that. People don't always need to know how problems are going to be solved. Sometimes, it's enough to know that their leader is confident he can do it.

Figuring all this out will take some time and effort. Some of it you will do yourself while driving your car and/or taking a shower. Much of it can be worked out with your key people while the idea itself is being thought through. And you can call meetings with your key team to specifically talk about "How Are We Going to Sell This Good Idea to the Rest of the Company?"

As you develop your strategy, stay relaxed and open. Make the assumption, going into the process that your idea will change along the way. If you insist that your original idea stay intact you will lose the support of some of your key people and you will probably end up with a weaker idea. You will also end up with an idea that is harder to sell.

Be confident about the basic validity of your idea but flexible about its particular manifestation. Keep in mind that your primary purpose is to improve the business. It's about growth and profits, not about you. And before the actual selling process begins, be sure you have done your homework. Ask yourself these critical questions:

1. "Is this idea one that will make things better for others (customers, constituents, clients, etc.), or am I pursuing it for some personal/selfish reason?"
2. "Have I given this idea a reasonable level of scrutiny? Have I subjected it to a critique by at least one person whose judgment I trust?"

Your answers will help you determine if you need to take your idea back to the drawing board, or modify your goals.

SELLING THE TROOPS

When it's time to actually sell the rank and file, speak with the certainty of someone who has done all the preliminary work you have done. Realize that no matter how extensively you prepare, sometime during the process of selling your idea you will be surprised with an objection or argument you didn't anticipate. If you expect this to happen you won't panic when it does. If the surprise comes during a presentation, say, "That is a good point, John. I'll get to it in a minute or two after I first clarify

> "Effective leaders are constantly reducing doubt in themselves and their followers. If every human being has some level of doubt, the key to leadership is to influence people to work at resolving their doubts thus raising them to higher levels of thinking and behaving."
> Steven M. Bornstein, Anthony F. Smith; The Leader of the Future.[24]

---

24 Bornstein, Steven M., Smith, Anthony F. contributors in **The Leader of the Future,** The Drucker Foundation, New York: 1996

the issue of..." This diversion will allow you to keep the momentum going while you try to think of a satisfactory answer. If you don't, don't sweat. Compliment the questioner for his intelligence. You may want to go so far as to say, "John has asked a very intelligent question, one for which I have no immediate answer. I'm going to think about it a bit and talk to some people. I'll have an answer for him and for you before [some timeframe].

Say this with conviction and you won't lose any converts.

And finally, keep this in mind. Your idea doesn't have to be perfect to succeed. In the busy, complex world that we live in, there are many problems and many solutions to those problems. The person who is ultimately successful is the person who can keep trying out ideas until he finds one that works.

In terms of leadership, that means you must retain control through the period of doubt so that your idea can be fully implemented. As I said, it doesn't have to be the perfect solution to work. It just needs to be good enough. But unless you maintain control, your idea won't get a chance to work. So prepare yourself, make clear statements, and establish doable, step-by-step objectives.

And never lose confidence. Keep in mind that your primary strength as a leader is your character—that you are genuinely committed to the betterment of the business. If your key people and the troops sense that, they will forgive you for almost anything else. So long as they think your idea can work, they will work with you.

Once leaders get their team excited about a new project or idea, the good ones create a detailed plan with specific deadlines to keep the momentum going. They use a 5 step process to create objectives and define tasks with realistic deadlines attached to them. Their plan is put in writing and communicated verbally to everyone involved.

#5: CREATING A PLAN AND ATTACHING A DEADLINE

"If everything's under control, you're going too slow."
~Mario Andretti

Your team is excited about a new project. Now you have to get them moving and keep them moving. They must remain energized and directed. They must be flexible and creative. They must overcome obstacles. To achieve all of this—and achieve it quickly—you need a detailed plan and a realistic set of deadlines for each member of your team.

Good leaders know that communicating the goal is just step one. Getting to success requires a plan—one that is well thought out, written down and developed into specific objectives. Furthermore, these objectives must be communicated clearly and have standards of quality and deadlines attached to them.

In *The Leader of the Future* Dave Ulrich calls this process "organizational capability."[25] He says that great leaders know how to create a plan of attack and use it to "shape, structure, implement and improve organizational processes to meet business goals." I agree. By creating a

---

25 Ulrich, Dave contributor in *The Leader of the Future*, The Drucker Foundation, New York: 1996.

specific plan and setting precise deadlines you are making it easier for your team to achieve the goal and implement your idea in the shortest time possible. And if your plan and deadlines are structured appropriately, you won't have to sacrifice quality.

HOW TO CREATE A SUCCESSFUL PLAN

So how do you create the right kind of plan that gives you timely completion and the highest quality?

Start at the end. That's right— you're going to work backwards. It's really quite simple, just follow five steps:

1. Starting from the end—the result you want—write down all the partial objectives you need to achieve along the way.
2. For each one of these objectives you should create a list of the specific tasks that need to be completed.
3. Next, identify who you think might do the best job of completing each task. In some cases you may want to name a second or even a third choice.
4. Now append a specific deadline to each task. Deadlines should be challenging but also realistic.

Before we continue, an important note about deadlines: resist all efforts (even from your superiors) to accept any deadline until you've had the chance to break down the project in the above manner. Only after determining the project's component parts and then figuring out how much time it will take to complete each part should you ever commit to a deadline.

This being said, as a person who likes to see things grow and change, I'm always pushing people to agree to fast deadlines. I'm happy when they do, but I'm also perfectly happy when they show me that a deadline I'm urging is unrealistic.

When it comes to deadlines, I'd rather get the disappointing news early on and then adjust to that. Most business people I know are like me in this regard. So when you have to agree on when you'll get the project completed, take the time to come up with a realistic answer.

5. Communicate orally and in writing your plan of action. Both explanations should include the following:

- The overall goal.
- The intermediate objectives.
- How each major task will advance the plan.
- Why certain people were selected to do certain tasks.
- How and why the deadlines were assigned.

If you fail to include just one of these specifics in your explanation, you could fall victim to what consultant and clinical psychologist Dr. Laurie Anderson calls "executive blah blah." This is executive speak which lacks concrete instruction and has no real meaning so it doesn't achieve results.

HOW TO BE SURE YOUR EMPLOYEES "GET IT"

However, even if you've explained your plan clearly and in detail, there may be some laggards who just don't get it. So watch for the warning signs. In *The Instant Consultant* from Executive Excellence Publishing, Dr. Anderson says there are ways to be sure team members understand the new plan.[26] She says if they "get it" they should:

- Ask you good questions.
- Be able to repeat to you or to someone else the new actions or results that are now expected of them. This includes repeating the first steps that they need to take as part of your plan.
- Exhibit genuine passion, excitement or discomfort when expectations for new action and change are announced.

I don't believe in handholding employees, but if you fear you've got a laggard or two on your hands, here's a quick way to know for sure. Why not ask *them* for help.

Ask them to summarize your plan and their role in it in an email to a co-worker or manager who wasn't in the meeting, copying you

---

26 Anderson, Dr. Laurie, *The Instant Consultant*, Executive Excellence Publishing, June 2002.

of course. This way you can make sure they have a clear understanding of the goal, what's expected of them and when. And if you find they don't, you can rectify it immediately. This little step can save you lots of headaches later on.

Your good employees should not have any problem putting a well-explained plan into action. And if you've followed the steps above and set realistic deadlines for each individual task, you'll know immediately who's having trouble and who isn't—it will be apparent in their work or lack there of.

#6: FOLLOWING UP

"You don't get points for predicting rain. You get points for building an ark."
~Louis J. Gerstner, Chairman and CEO of IBM

From a distance, the business world may look like a chessboard of clever ideas—but up close and personal, it's a rugby field of getting things done. At one point in my career I looked at my daily-task lists and was struck by how much time I was spending in the unpleasant, sometimes odious, capacity of persuading others to act. I spent 60 to 70 percent of my working hours encouraging, badgering, and sometimes threatening perfectly competent business managers by memo, meeting, fax, e-mail, or phone.

And to think—I considered myself an idea man.

It's true that many of the great business successes I've enjoyed have had, at their core, a good idea. And I enjoy brainstorming immensely. I am also a sucker for the plaudits that come when your big idea works.

But when I examine the history of my business life as it really was on a daily, hourly basis, and not how it appears from the distance of casual reflection, I realize that it was the follow up, not the great ideas that was the biggest part of my success.

FOLLOWING UP CAN MAKE OR BREAK YOUR IDEA

In past chapters we've talked about creating the big ideas and then developing a plan to execute them. But success in business doesn't end there. All true business leaders realize that their responsibility for projects doesn't end after tasks have been delegated and deadlines set. They know that it's necessary to push team members periodically during the process by sending memos and making phone calls.

First is the idea. Next is the plan. Then most of the rest of it is pushing, pushing, pushing.

HOW TO FOLLOW UP

Here's a good way to push your plan into action. Take out your calendar and mark down all of the intermediate deadlines you've set for each complex task. Rotate this list through your own monthly to-do file so that you can prod and push your team forward ceaselessly as the project progresses.

And this is most important: you must follow up on each deadline with a note.

Next month send another note. If you receive objections respond politely and keep sending notes until the project is finished. And when the last deadline rolls around, phone or e-mail the responsible party at 5 p.m. if you don't get what you've been promised.

Serious follow up involves something else too, something much more than sending a series of urgent reminders. A friend of mine recently offered me some great insight on this subject. He said, "Instead of giving your people two dozen great ideas and then pestering them with "Where's this at?" memos, focus on the single most important idea and follow up in a more serious way."

TAKE FOLLOWING UP TO THE NEXT LEVEL

He's right. To ensure success you must be prepared to take your personal involvement to the next level. This type of follow up is the willingness to set aside time to make sure the objective is clearly understood, to discuss and review the plan for accomplishing it, and to help brainstorm solutions to any problems. This is truly a secret to strong leadership, and though it's relatively simple it's rarely followed.

When I think back over my career, it's clear to me that most of the big jobs accomplished by my businesses were done after I dug in and got seriously involved. If you do the same you'll find the really effective big ideas are few and far between, and the thing that moves a business forward is the actualization of smaller ideas. And that's okay. One hour's worth of good ideas each month is more than most businesses can handle anyway.

DO YOU DO ENOUGH FOLLOW UP?

Spend a few minutes this week candidly assessing your work. What are you spending most of your time doing?

1. Coming up with ideas?
2. Handling/solving unrelated problems?
3. Pushing people to make things happen?

You have to do some of each to succeed. But if you are spending most of your time brainstorming and/or solving unrelated problems, you are probably not making the progress you could be. Focus more on following up on the status of your idea or project, and push until everything happens!

#7: CREATE A CULTURE OF ACCOUNTABILITY

"Few things help an individual more than to place responsibility upon him, and to let him know that you trust him."
~Booker T. Washington

In an interview with *Fast Company Magazine,* management guru Tom Peters said that the world of business had been changed by the collapse of the Internet bubble and the wake of corporate fraud and corruption that followed. He predicted that the future would be an "Age of No-Bull Performance."

Peters had one recommendation for executives who want to succeed in the "real new economy." Play less and do more. Leaders must do more than provide vision, he said, they must deliver performance. I agree. In the preceding chapters we talked about how to make your business dreams come true. Create a realistic, exciting goal. Develop a detailed plan to achieve it. Follow up on that plan by interacting with all the key people on a regular basis.

But there's something else you have to do—especially if you expect your business to grow and you want your job to become more interesting. You have to develop a strong sense of accountability among your staff.

WHAT DOES ACCOUNTABILITY REALLY MEAN?

Accountability means that everyone on your team feels responsible for the successful outcome of the project at hand and also the overall health and wealth of the division (or business) for which he works. That's a lot to expect from a worker, but you can get it if you want. The foundation of accountability is trust. You should give each employee as much trust as he needs to complete the job. If, for example, you tell Susan that it's her job to create the advertising brochure, you have to allow her the freedom and authority (within predetermined, reasonable limits) to do it.

If you have difficulty trusting people and like to micromanage your employees you will have trouble making people accountable. You can tell them that they are responsible for a certain part of the project, but if they know you will be looking over their shoulder every day or two, they will never feel responsible. Not only will they not feel accountable, they will probably feel resentful.

TRUST, BUT NOT BEYOND MERIT

I don't believe in trusting people beyond their merit. Blind trust is foolish in your social life and financially perilous in business. But if you want to get a lot of work done you will have to rely on a team of people to work hard and smart for you, and to accomplish that you are going to have to give each person enough trust to feel accountable for the job you've asked him to do.

ENCOURAGE EMPLOYEES TO THINK

You should also encourage your employees to think for themselves. Rather than play the role of Mr. Answer for Every Question, try a little circumvention now and then. When someone asks you how to solve some important new problem, resist the urge to be brilliant and say, "What do you think we should do?" A habit of challenging your team members with questions will teach you a great deal about their capabilities, much more than you'd ever learn being Mr. Answer, and you may surprise yourself by how many useful, new ideas they come up with.

KEEP YOUR TEAM INFORMED

Another important part of creating a "culture of accountability" (to use an odious cliché) is keeping team members informed of any significant changes in your thinking. Business projects are fluid things. They can't be expected to follow the course of direction envisioned at the outset. When unanticipated problems and challenges arise, you must react to them. There are four things you must make sure you do when passing along this new information, you must let everyone know:

1. What has happened.
2. How it affects the project.
3. What your response is.
4. How your response may affect their responsibilities.

Taking the time to attend to this relatively simple, four-part protocol will save you a great deal of grief, accelerate progress and accentuate team feeling of being involved and responsible.

This is the pleasant side of creating a culture of accountability—good planning, consideration and communication. There is a tough part too—handling mistakes, miscalculations and failures.

HANDLING FAILURE: HOW YOU SHOULD DO IT

In an accountable system, when things go awry someone is to blame. Blame is a dirty word today, but it shouldn't be. Blame means equating a problem with an individual. It's not always fair to blame one person for a situation that involved many people and quite possibly events beyond anyone's control, but in an accountable system blame must nevertheless be given.

You don't need to throw stones, although you may sometimes want to. But you do need to identify one person as blameworthy. The individual to blame is the person responsible for the process that failed. He took on the job of getting it done. It didn't get done. He's responsible. I've been using the word blame to make a point, but a better word is responsible.

Responsible means blameworthy but without the connotations of shame.

Here's a 4 step plan to handle failures or problems when they arise:

1. Locate the responsible party.
2. Tell him that he is responsible for fixing the problem.
3. Allow little or no time for explanations, excuses, finger pointing or hair pulling. Just focus on the solution.
4. Make sure he accepts responsibility for it.

THERE'S A PLACE FOR GUILT

A word on guilt. If someone screws up, they should feel guilty. If they don't feel guilty you should try to make them feel so. Guilt is a very useful and enabling emotion. It motivates us to do better in the future. Don't make people feel guilty when they were merely wrong, or overly optimistic or inexperienced, but do make them feel guilty if they were lazy or sloppy or dishonest.

Blame, responsibility and guilt—they all play a part in creating an environment where people are accountable.

DON'T FORGET TO PRAISE GREAT WORK

The last but not least important way of creating an accountable business team is to praise individuals for performance that is beyond expectation and celebrate victories, little and big, with the team as a whole.

An accountable team is an invaluable asset. Creating one takes planning, thoughtfulness, communication, and toughness but it also takes a happy heart.

Good leaders recognize the importance of practicing all the skills essential to leadership—one of the most important being persuasion. They understand that by using these skills and analyzing their strong and weak areas they can work systematically to become better leaders.

#8: PRACTICE MAKES PERFECT

"Practice means to perform, over and over again in the face of all obstacles, some act of vision, of faith, of desire. Practice is a means of inviting the perfection desired."
~Martha Graham

If you want to become a better leader you have to practice your leadership skills in the same way an aspiring pianist sits down and practices his chords. Masters of any skill become so only when the skill becomes second nature—almost like breathing—and this requires repetition after repetition.

But there's a good and a bad way to practice. You can't rush through, you must do it right. Taking the time to perform your skills the right way is the key to mastery. Don't practice mistakes. Practice perfection.

PRACTICE YOUR PASSION

Gary North of Reality Check fame believes strongly in doing work that you care about. He says that if you pick a field of work that really interests you,—"something that ignites your imagination and makes you feel like you are doing some good—your chances of sticking with it will be much greater".

The greatest enemy to success, he says, is loss of passion. And losing your love of something is most likely if your enthusiasm for it is shallow. (In discussing my own career, he once advised me that I should write only about those things that I'd write about if I weren't paid for the writing. That shook me up a little. Now I know he was absolutely correct.)

Next to passion, tenacity is the greatest virtue. Stick with what you care about even when it doesn't seem as though you can make it work. So long as you can pay your bills and feed your family, stick with it. If it's important enough to demand your devotion, it is worth sacrificing for.

Gradually, North says, you'll make your progress. You don't have to necessarily do anything brilliant. Just keep doing the sensible things and eventually you'll find your way. 80% of success is just showing up, Woody Allen once said. Gary North agrees.

"Start at the bottom," North says, "Scrub the toilets. Do the work that nobody else wants until the system depends on you. Keep learning. Keep improving yourself." I think this advice holds true no matter where you are in your career, whether you're just starting out or whether you've been in your industry for decades.

WHAT SKILLS DO *YOU* NEED TO BECOME A BETTER LEADER?

Choose a career you care about. This will give you passion—the fuel you'll use to push yourself through all the trials and tribulations of becoming a great leader.

But passion is not enough. You need specific skills. The following quiz will give you a quick assessment of your strength and weakness in terms of leadership skills: Answer the next six questions with one of the following: "inadequate", "competent", or "masterful."

1. How well do you know the important secrets of your business?
2. How good are you at sharing that knowledge with your key people?
3. How effective are you at inspiring others to follow your ideas?

4. How demanding are you in terms of getting others to reach their goals and objectives?
5. How good are you at following up?
6. How strong are you at coming up with useful, new ideas?

Now tally up your score. Give yourself one point for every "inadequate" answer, two points for every "competent" answer, and five points for every "masterful" answer.

If you scored more than 20, you are a natural leader. You need to focus primarily on your greatest leadership strength and try to fix your greatest leadership weakness. Look at your answers to the above questions to determine this focus.

If you scored between 10 and 20, you have great potential. The most important thing you can do is to commit yourself to being better—make it a goal. Specifically you should work to strengthen your industry knowledge and your ability to come up with good ideas about what needs to be done. Work to strengthen your communication skills. Practice the goal setting process of creating goals, setting deadlines and following up. The techniques you're learning about in this book will help you do all of these.

If you scored below 10, you have your work cut out for you. But it's never hopeless. You should eat, sleep and breathe the traits and skills of good leaders you'll find in this book. Practice the process of coming up with big ideas. Learn how you can inspire others to follow your vision and carry it out. You'll need to strengthen your communication skills, and practice the goal setting process of creating goals, setting deadlines and following up.

EVERY MINUTE OF PRACTICE PAYS OFF

Exercising leadership is a complicated skill and like most complicated skills (playing basketball or chess, for example) it takes a lot of time and a considerable amount of coaching to become competent

Every good leader knows that he can never be good enough at persuasion. Whether his job is to convince a hundred thousand shareholders that his five year restructuring plan is worth a billion dollars of their money or to convince his personal assistant to improve his handwriting, knowing how to convince people that your ideas are worth following—that's the greatest leadership skill.

and even masterful.

In all human endeavors, there are four levels of accomplishment.

1. Incompetence

Regardless of how smart or gifted you are, to learn a new skill you must go through a period of not knowing—of taking the baby steps and stumbling. This is the very necessary stage of incompetence. Being incompetent is nothing to be ashamed of. Not trying to learn something because you are afraid to show incompetence is.

2. Competence

If you persist in your learning, you will eventually arrive at a level of skill that is competent for most situations. For example, you will be able to play the piano at parties, dance at weddings, or write an effective business letter. It takes time to become competent. I've suggested, half seriously, that it's always the same amount of time regardless of the skill: 1,000 hours (with a 30% discount if you are lucky enough to have masterful instruction).

3. Mastery

Most people stop learning after they achieve competence. They know enough not to get fired, laughed at, or rejected (in other words, enough to avoid pain), but they have no desire to go beyond that. The few people who are not satisfied with merely "good" push on and continue to practice and learn for years and years. At some point (and my guesstimate for that is after about 5,000 hours), because of all that extra work and especially because of that extra attention, they achieve a level of accomplishment that distinguishes them from their competent peers. They become masters of their skill. One person out of a hundred competent people achieves mastery.

4. Virtuosity

The virtuoso is not only extremely focused, determined, hard-working, and persistent, but also divinely gifted. He is the one master out of a hundred masters that has a genius for the skill that allows him to be a world-class performer. Even so, the virtuoso must put in the time—I'd guess a minimum of 25,000 hours—working at it. Like Michael Jordan, Fred Astaire, Bill Clinton (well . . . maybe not Bill Clinton), and others of that ilk.

Back to you. I think this is roughly true of leadership. Since the individual skills of leadership (the ability to analyze problems, brainstorm solutions, communicate them clearly and stir up support) are required in many aspects of our lives, many people come into their profession with already developed leadership skills. Others reach their 60s without ever having made much progress in this area.

Let's assume that you want to reach a level of mastery. How long will it take you to put in 5000 hours of practice? If we are talking about a 40-hour week, 5,000 hours is two and a half years. If you devote an hour a day, it will take you 15 years. If you start at age 20, by 35 you will be an expert. For something that takes an hour a day, that's not too long to wait."

Ideally you should start young. But even if you don't you can still become a leader in your chosen field. The experience you already have will count for something. But you still need to put in a lot of hours—maybe 3,000 or 4,000, depending on what you know and what you need to do to become a leader in your trade.

To get that time in faster, you need to find more time to devote to your goal of becoming a better leader. That may mean cutting back on your responsibilities, staying up later, or (better yet) getting up extra early to work on your skills. Break your necessary tasks down into years, months, and weeks. Then put them on your daily "to-do" list and start to feel the progress you are making.

The best leaders realize that hard work is more important than talent and skill any day of the week. Those who aspire to rise to the top not only work harder and longer than others, they work smarter. They use their time wisely and they network in and out of their department to gain the trust of others. They get involved in the right projects and make their good work known by sending memos to the decision makers.

CHAPTER 11:
HOW TO GET PROMOTED

"Opportunity is missed by most because it is dressed in overalls and looks like work."
~Thomas J. Edison

What's the best way to surpass your peers and put yourself on the fast track to a leadership position?

The answer is simple: Work harder than they do. And work on what's most important to the business.

If that sounds daunting, consider this: Most people don't work very hard. Some people spend their time doing as little as they possibly can. Most do stay busy, but they are not always very productive. They write long memos, discuss issues that don't need much discussion, contest insignificant points, and attend to the tedium. But only a very few apply themselves long and hard to the critical business challenges.

Doing simply a modest amount of extra work (an hour a day, say) will put you beyond both the terminally slothful and the lump-along middle crowd. Add to that a dash of ambition (volunteering for important projects, networking with people who can support you, getting a mentor, etc.) and you will almost certainly rise to the top quarter or third of any working group. This will get you into a good management position but if you want to go all the way to the top, if you want to become director or C.E.O., then you are going to have to work even harder and smarter because you'll be competing not against ordinary employees but against others who are, like you, ambitious and hardworking.

Don't underestimate your fellow workers. Chances are they are as smart and talented as you, with the same (or more) basic resources. They may even have better contacts. But there is one thing they don't have more of and that is time.

USE YOUR TIME WISELY

If you can use your time more effectively than they use theirs, you will move ahead of them. It's all a matter of focusing your extra time and energy on what most benefits the business. This is a big secret, one most employees don't understand. Nor is it well known by the top performers, many of whom are so consumed with their own futures, their own ideas and their own rewards that they have little time to think about what's best for the business.

By focusing on the business first you can do better than someone who is smarter, richer, and luckier than you so long as you are willing to work harder than he does.

As a colleague and friend said to me one night, "Life isn't fair. When it comes to money, beauty, intelligence, and talent, the distribution is uneven and arbitrary. But one thing we all have an equal amount of is time. We each have 24 hours a day. Even the length of life you get is not fair, but the 24 hours you have each day is the same for everyone—and what you do with those hours will determine your success and happiness."

People who rise to the top work long hours, but not excessively long. They are at their desks early, at least an hour before others, and they stay later—though it may be only a half-hour later. But what they do best is work harder when they work.

They do the necessary things first, even if they are difficult. They learn what they need to know and don't waste business time learning unimportant stuff. They are willing to harass and cajole, tease and criticize, flatter and pout to get the job done.

They spend a few minutes every morning organizing their days and a little while every Monday morning planning their week. They select their tasks based on what will achieve their goals, not on what happens to end up in their in boxes. They manage their jobs; they don't let their jobs manage them.

Hard work is a lot of, well, hard work. But if you break every job down into little, easy—to—handle pieces you can accomplish an extraordinary amount. And once you get into the habit of working harder and smarter than the people you compete with, your success is guaranteed.

HOW TO GET NOTICED FOR A PROMOTION

According to Saul Gellerman in his book Motivation *In The Real World*, when you get recommended for a promotion, your superiors are betting their reputations on you.[27] To make them take that risk, you need to do more than just do a good job. You need to do three more things.

1. Distinguish yourself from all of the other good performers.
2. Become known outside the immediate context of your job.
3. Learn how to manage your luck.

To distinguish yourself, you have to make it clear that you're not just a good whatever. You have to demonstrate competence in a broad range of tasks and a broad intelligence. The better you are at what you are doing now, the greater will be the tendency to typecast you by your present job.

Next, get to know as many people outside your department as possible. Use coffee breaks, get-togethers, and meetings to make your

---

27 Gellerman, Saul, *Motivation In The Real World*, Random House, 1995.

presence known and to get to know others. Show how nice you are, but display your competence too.

Each new contact is an opportunity for several more. Once you've established a rapport with someone, get him to introduce you to his colleagues or even his boss. Create your own personal, powerful internal network on every corporate level. Keep in mind that to successfully climb the ranks, you need the support of subordinates and colleagues as well as superiors.

You can learn to manage your luck the way a good infielder readies himself for a ball that may or may not be hit toward him. The infielder thinks through what he should do if the ball comes high or low, to the left or the right, so he will not have to think as the ball races toward him.

DEMONSTRATE YOUR ABILITY

To Gellerman's recommendations, I would add the following: You should try to whatever extent possible to demonstrate the skills of the job you are seeking as soon as you realize you want it. You want to show the world that you are capable of doing the job you seek well, and there's no better way to do that than by starting to do the relevant tasks BEFORE the job opens up.

How do you show the world you can do the job? First and most obviously, volunteer to help the current jobholder. A job worth having is usually complex and demanding. That means the person whose job you want will probably feel, at times at least, swamped. How could he resist your pleasant proposition to do the chores he doesn't have time for?

He may refuse your offer if he doesn't trust you. For example, if he wants to keep his job and gets the sense that you want to take it from him, expect resistance. So, if your plan is to replace him, you need to be very careful. But if he is moving on and you are hoping to succeed him, it should be easy to ask him for work. Ask for the grunge work first. The interesting stuff will come later.

Remember, the most important factor in getting ahead is to gain the trust of the people you work with—your subordinates, your colleagues, and your superiors. And you can't possibly get the confidence of all three groups unless you merit it. In short, the way to gain trust is to be trustworthy. I am talking about respecting the fundamental unwritten rule of hierarchy: "If you support my position, and you prove yourself to be superior, when it is time for me to move upstairs, I'll recommend you to replace me . . . but only if I can trust you to continue to support me."

IDENTIFY THE PERSON IN CHARGE

One more thing: Identify the superior who is really in charge of your career. This may or may not be your immediate superior. It should be, but in a broken structure, it may be the person above him.

HAVE INTEGRITY

When it comes to self-preservation, people are at their smartest. They listen with their full attention. They watch what you do. They overhear what you say to others. So be careful. And make up your mind that you will have integrity.

GET INVOLVED IN THE *RIGHT* PROJECTS

One good idea recommended by Jeffrey J. Fox in *How to Become CEO*, is to try to get involved in projects that are important, visible, or "the pet projects of senior people."[28] If you don't already know what those projects are, you can find out by simply asking. Ask your boss. Ask your boss's colleagues. Ask your company's C.E.O., C.F.O., or whomever.

Identify two or three such problems and then choose one that you'd be interested in working on. Present yourself to the person in charge of dealing with that problem and offer to help in any way possible. Don't be pushy, be enthusiastic. And don't be demanding, instead

---

28 Fox, Jeffrey J. *How to Become CEO: The Rules for Rising to the Top of Any Organization*, Hyperion Press, October 1998

be obliging, almost servile.

To establish a company—wide reputation for being an up-and-comer, you need two or three large feathers in your cap. You'll get one feather for each such voluntary effort.

GET THE WORD OUT WITHOUT BRAGGING

As you go about putting in these extra hours, be sure to document them with casual memos to everyone possible. Be discrete, but be ubiquitous.

One caveat: Try never to claim more than is just. In fact, try not to boast about your successes at all. You can get the word out merely by talking about the projects to the people that count. Ask for their opinions. Share ideas that might be helpful to them. Get into the mix.

Let the key people know how good you are without seeming to want them to know. This is essential in *everything* work related that you do.

It has always been my policy to give my boss more value than he has a right to expect, and to let him know whenever I do something good. If you are not doing the same things in your work life you should. Or else someone who hasn't half your talent and provides less than half the value you provide may get a promotion over you. And why? Because the boastful, self-aggrandizing S.O.B. is willing to sing his own praises.

It's so unfair! Your bosses should be smarter than that! Unfortunately, it doesn't work that way. Remember you don't have to be a braggart to get the word out. You need only be brave enough to start a conversation.

PUT THE BUSINESS FIRST

And finally I want to come back to something I said before. Make sure that everything you do and every decision you make is done for the betterment of the business. Don't worry about your own short-term concerns. And never, ever get yourself ensnarled in office politics. Show your leadership skills by not getting involved in anything negative or distracting. Be the person who is solely focused on what counts—the growth and development of the enterprise.

If you do that and follow some of the other suggestions made in

---

OTHER PROMOTION TIPS:

- Know what you want and where you want to be. Make it clear to your superiors.
- Ask people in power for guidance.
- Network with those below you and across from you professionally.
- Constantly work to improve your core skills and never refuse a training opportunity.
- Don't turn down any opportunity to lead or be promoted.
- Be willing to take risks.[29]

---

this chapter your future as a top leader will be virtually assured.

---

29 Lavinski, Rosemary "Use it or Lose Out," *Black Enterprise*, February 2001.

CHAPTER 12:
THE POWER OF DELEGATION

"If you don't know what to do with many of the papers piled on your desk, stick a dozen colleagues' initials on them and pass them along. When in doubt, route."
~Malcolm S. Forbes

There's something to be said for doing a project or task yourself—you know it has been done right. But if you want to be a strong leader you must do what Malcolm Forbes does and learn to give up control over certain tasks. You must learn to delegate. Delegation is essential to leadership because it frees up time for the things you should be focusing on—like improving your business.

As a general rule, you want to delegate as much work as you possibly can. This is an absolute requirement for a growing business. As sales increase, so do problems—small problems, medium problems, and big problems. Your job as a leader is to delegate all the small and medium-sized problems to subordinates so you have time to concentrate on the big ones yourself.

If you are lucky enough to have a superstar working for you, you'll

113

be able to delegate some of the big problems too. That is exactly how it should be. The senior, experienced people handle the newest, most challenging issues, while the more routine stuff gets worked on by the less experienced, less knowledgeable employees who can, nevertheless, do a fine job with it.

WHAT TO DELEGATE

Here are some guidelines I use to delegate projects. If the project can be completed successfully by someone else . . . delegate it. You should also delegate everything that is beneath your level of skill and responsibility, like those small and medium-sized problems. If you have people working under you you'll have thousands of opportunities to get rid of work and responsibilities. You can and should pass on as many routine jobs as possible. The best way to do this is to make them a normal part of the delegate's workload.

In his book *How to Delegate,* Robert Heller says being able to analyze the importance of a project and the skill it will take to complete, is the first step to effective delegation.[30] I agree. And key to this step is also recognizing what you should *never* delegate. As the leader of your profit center don't pass on high priority projects that will reflect badly on you if there's a mistake made somewhere. These projects can almost always be placed into one of two categories:

1. The ultimate responsibility for sales
2. The ultimate responsibility for product quality

Putting yourself in charge of generating sales is smart because it keeps you in the primary position. (The man who holds the cash spigot gets credit for the cash flow.) It's also smart because—if things ever turn against you—the skills you will hone as sales honcho will enable you to find another job or even start your own knock-off business.

And you want to maintain control over the quality of your prod-

---

30 Heller, Robert, Hindle, Tim *How To Delegate*, DK Publishing, January 1997.

uct because it's crucial to your ongoing success in the marketplace. If standards start to deteriorate—even if the change is incremental and hardly noticeable—it can kill your business. Remember, there are basically two reasons why businesses fail. Either they forget how to make the initial sale or they allow their products to become noticeably worse than the other, similar products in the marketplace. If both things happen simultaneously, the business is almost sure to fail—and fast. Because strong leaders are effective delegators, they're able to keep their eyes on the big picture and not let this happen.

"HOW TO DELEGATE"

In *How to Delegate*, Robert Heller lists 4 simple steps to effective delegation:

1. Appointment
2. Briefing
3. Control
4. Appraisal

MAKE YOUR APPOINTMENT

After you've decided which tasks you'll pass along, Heller says you should sort them. Break them down and figure out what will be required to complete each one. I agree. This is so you can determine who best to "appoint" or delegate the task to.

Heller brings up another valid point here. He recommends going against an often natural instinct to always delegate only to those employees who know how to do the task at hand. I agree. Instead you should use delegation as an opportunity to teach your employees new skills. This will surely pay off later. Plus, by keeping your employees challenged you will give them a sense of self-worth which will be reflected in their work for you.

ARE YOU A GOOD DELEGATOR? TEST YOURSELF!

Do you ...

1. Define the job's objectives to your delegate and specify what you would consider to be "success" before you begin?

2. Tell your delegate why you chose him? Identify a strength he has that is important to finishing the job?

3. Set a deadline and explain to him why that deadline is important?

4. Require intermediate reporting or regular checkups?

5. Let him do his work without a lot of interference?

6. Make sure he gets the credit—and the glory—if he succeeds?

BRIEF YOUR DELEGATE

The next step is briefing. After you delegate you must "clearly define" the task. You should not only provide instructions but offer any extra training or coaching. Heller's right here too, but this should only be necessary in the beginning. After a time your employee should be able to complete the task or job successfully without any coaching from you. And when it comes time for your employee to delegate the task to someone else, make your employee responsible for instructing his or her colleague. As leader, you shouldn't devote any time to re-teaching the task ever again.

MONITOR YOUR DELEGATE

The last two of Heller's steps are control and appraisal. These include monitoring the delegate's work and coming up with suggestions that can improve performance. Heller recommends using regular sessions to review the delegate's performance. I think this is essential to make sure no mistakes are made . . . mistakes that could ultimately reflect on you. However, a word of caution: Don't look over your employee's shoulder so much that you might as well have just done the task yourself. Like me, you'll probably have very specific opinions about how the project should be completed . . . you'll have to learn to be flexible to a point.

It's also important to recognize your employee for a job well done, and as a 'reward' delegate jobs with larger responsibilities attached. This will benefit both you and your employees.

Some of the best leaders have been mentored at some point in their careers. Many credit their mentors with helping them hone the skills they used to succeed. These leaders understand how important it is to find a mentor and establish a beneficial relationship based on learning.

CHAPTER 13:
ACHIEVE MORE WITH A MENTOR

"It can be no dishonor to learn from others when they speak good sense."
~Sophocles, Antigone

A man looks back on his life and says, "I wish I knew then what I know now."

It can take a decade or more to become a great leader, but you can shorten your learning curve—even drastically curtail it—by using a mentor.

With the advice, experience and support of an experienced person in your field can avoid the most common mistakes you are likely to make; you overcome the stickiest problems and find short cuts to success. It doesn't really matter where you are along your career path, getting yourself a good mentor will be enormously valuable for you.

A survey commissioned by the Elliot Leadership Institute at Johnson & Wales University confirms this. For this particular study, researchers surveyed senior executives and middle managers in the food service and hospitality industry about leadership competencies. What they discovered was that leaders who had been mentored felt the experience invaluable. They said their mentor helped them to build all kinds of leadership skills including decision-making, strategic thinking, planning, coaching and effective management of others.[31]

In *Early to Rise* I've often talked about the mentors in my own business life. From Leo, my first post college boss, I learned the importance of persistence and dogged determination. Leo once had me call Honda Motors more than 100 times to convince them to give us a new engine after the one we had had died from lack of oil. We hadn't a single, sensible argument in our favor but that didn't stop Leo from pushing me. A hundred phone calls later, having gotten all the way to the top, the Honda executive leadership decided they had wasted too much time on us and gave in. I didn't feel good about getting something we didn't deserve, but I never forgot that lesson in persistence.

From Joel, my second major mentor, I learned a great deal. The first lesson he taught me—by firing the lady who wanted me fired—was that a good leader needs to surround himself with the strongest people he can find. Another lesson I learned soon thereafter had to do with the fundamental nature of business. "Until we make a sale," Joel explained patiently, "nothing else happens."

From Bill, a client, partner and part-time mentor, I discovered—relatively late in my career—two important business secrets that have made me a better leader: I no longer feel compelled to solve every problem put at my feet. I've watched Bill ignore countless squabbles and come out much the better for it. Before getting involved in a dispute these days I ask myself, "Can these people eventually come up with a satisfactory solution themselves?" If the answer is affirmative, I do nothing.

I'm a big believer in product quality. Having mastered the secrets of selling through my relationship with Joel I tended to underestimate the importance of the product. I was one of those marketers who actually wanted to sell snow to Eskimos. In working with Bill, whose sole focus is always on quality, I've seen how much better a business becomes (and easier to lead) when you stress quality.

---

31 "The business case for leadership development: part 2 in a series of research findings from the EU" *Nation's Restaurant News*, August 4, 2003.

You probably have no idea what you need to learn to make the next leap forward in your career. But someone who's been there and done it before probably does. Getting the help of someone who can help you will make a very big difference in your future. The sooner you get to it, the faster things will start to change and improve.

FINDING YOUR MENTOR

Look around your industry and think about some of the big success stories. Write down the names of five successful business leaders who retired within the past two to five years. This time frame is important, because if they've been retired for any longer they could be out of touch.

Any sooner and they're not bored enough yet with retirement to miss thinking about work.

Write each of these five people a short letter expressing genuine admiration for their careers. Compliment them on specific achievements. Then ask for advice on your own career.

Offer an invitation to go to lunch, or if location is a problem, ask for a 15 minute phone call. And don't, I repeat don't, offer any compensation. Odds are at least one of the five will respond positively, and give you a little of his or her time. If you find you get along, you've got yourself a mentor.

MAKING THE MOST OF YOUR RELATIONSHIP WITH YOUR MENTOR

Once you've found your mentor make a list of goals for your relationship. What do you want out of it?

What do you feel you need to learn? What can this person best teach you? These are the goals you'll work on with your mentor.

Mentorship experts recommend meeting with your mentor either in person or over the phone on a regular basis.[32]

---

32 Braley, Sarah J.F. "Finding a good mentor: who to turn to for valuable career advice, and how to make the most of the relationship." *Meetings & Conventions*, July, 2002.

Prior to your conversation, outline what you want to achieve from your time together. Keep track of your progress with your mentor. Are you achieving what you set out too? It's important that you set and monitor your goals because your mentor most likely won't.

HOW TO MAKE SURE YOU'VE GOT A GOOD MENTOR

A mentorship is a relationship built on learning. Your mentor should be your learning coach: someone you can talk to and trust. A good mentor should provide you with advice, feedback and support. He should help you focus on your goals and give you direction that helps you succeed more quickly than you could alone.

A good mentor should help you learn the secrets to success in your industry and field of expertise. That's why finding one in your field is so important. Your mentor should offer advice on skills they've found valuable. He should counsel you concerning various opportunities in your industry and different paths to success.

According to an article in *Black Enterprise* good mentors won't tell you how to do your job. They should give you feedback and share their personal experiences, but not inundate you with lots of unsolicited advice. And good mentors shouldn't be making decisions for you that you could have made for yourself. "Your mentor is not a savior" as the article says.[33] I agree. If you're going to learn from your mentor, he can't come up with every single solution for you, nor should you expect him too. Your mentor should act as a sounding board and as a trusted advisor and counselor. I like the way business writer Ron Yudd put it in his opinion column, mentors "hold the flashlight so others can see the path."[34]

RESPECT THE MENTOR-MENTEE RELATIONSHIP

If you want to maintain your relationship with your mentor, you must recognize his value and reward him for it. Keep in mind—the

33 Clarke, Robyn D. "Give Good Guidance", *Black Enterprise*, November 2000.
34 Yudd, Ron, "Real-life mentoring lights way for future leaders" *Restaurant News*, July 28, 2003.

kind of advice he is giving you is likely to have the most profound effect on your career. Although you can't measure the value of any specific suggestion (i.e., "Stop spending so much time on this fulfillment project. Get to work on improving your space ads.") you can bet that in the long run the effect will be very significant.

Show him you appreciate what he is doing for you. Tell him, in specific terms, what you have learned from him and thank him every time he meets with you. Remember, the psychological reward of knowing he is helping you succeed is his primary reward for his time. That said, offer to compensate him financially.

How much? That's up to you. Pay him no more than you feel comfortable paying him and no less than he thinks is fair. If you can't find a number in between those two figures, find another mentor.

One of my current mentors, Sid, gets a check of several thousand dollars every time I spend time with him. On a per-hour basis he's extremely well paid, but for the help he gives me in making key leadership and wealth-building decisions, the $30,000 to $40,000 a year I invest in him is a bargain.

[KEY POINT]

Jack Welch is known as one of the most successful business leaders. One reason is that he found an innovative way to increase productivity. He created an exciting vision people could believe in and he promoted the flow of ideas, then he simply asked people to work more quickly—and they did. This chapter takes a look at how Jack succeeded.

CHAPTER 14:
MAKE YOUR COMPANY BETTER AND MORE PRODUCTIVE TODAY

"You can't steal second base and keep one foot on first."
~Author unknown

When Jack Welch took over as CEO of GE, he surprised shareholders and industry analysts by announcing that before the end of his tenure the flagging industrial giant would climb back from near bankruptcy and become No.1 or No.2 in every market it was in. At the time, Welch's claim was considered arrogant. But within 10 years he had done just what he said he would do. To achieve this spectacular business feat, Welch took three actions that characterize great leaders:

1. He created an exciting vision, one that his workers and associates could be proud of.
2. He communicated his vision so well that it became a corporate mantra.
3. He broke down inter-company communication boundaries to increase the flow of ideas.

These actions took care of the GE organization itself. His people were motivated. They had a goal they could follow. They understood what was expected of them and knew how to talk about it with one another.

To meet his aggressive goals of growth and profitability Welch introduced "quickness" as a corporate-wide business goal—a "Eureka!" moment for me. He told GE's employees, "We want to do everything we do quicker than we do it now. And if you help us, we will reward you."

It was a brilliant idea. Usually, managers try to manipulate their workers into working harder, longer, and faster. Jack Welch simply asked them to do it. But he made his request a welcome challenge by establishing it as a company goal. This may seem simple but it's really revolutionary. By establishing the general concept of speed as a corporate goal (rather than, say, a specific target for production or customer service), he made doing almost anything faster a worthy objective. You can imagine how this might have spread through every department and division of GE. And those who were successful in doing things faster were rewarded and encouraged to do more.

The result was reported to be (and must have been) a great increase in efficiency and productivity. New protocols were established, and cumbersome and outdated practices were eliminated. Quickness can improve your profits in at least three ways: It reduces labor and energy costs, it eliminates inefficiencies (which have their own ancillary costs), and it improves morale and has a carryover effect on the productivity of everyone affected by it. Instead of finagling your people into moving more quickly, simply ask them to. They, not you, know where the productivity gaps are. Give them a chance to breach those gaps (and a reward for doing so) and your business will prosper.

PUT JACK WELCH'S IDEA TO WORK
IN YOUR OPERATION

There are 5 things you can do to use Jack Welch's idea successfully in your organization:

1. Spend some time thinking or rethinking your primary business goal. Discuss it with a few trusted colleagues to test it out.

2. Once you are comfortable with it, announce it formally to the troops. (For a more extensive explanation of steps 1 and 2 see Chapter 10, #1-8.)

3. Every time you meet with a manger thereafter, find a way to bring it into the conversation. Do that until they start talking about it.

4. Once the vision is established, introduce the idea of speed. Do so by writing a memo to your employees explaining how this idea works and asking for their help.

5. Work with your employees to establish a reward system for successfully implementing the "quickness" idea.

You can also implement Welch's idea in your own life and use it to accomplish whatever goals you've set for yourself. Just identify the tasks you perform each and every day and figure out how you can spend less time doing them without sacrificing quality.

PART THREE

POWER UP YOUR COMMUNICATION SKILLS

CHAPTER 15:

THE ART OF CRITICISM . . . THE SKILL OF PRAISE: HOW GOOD LEADERS USE BOTH TO THEIR ADVANTAGE

"If you haven't got anything nice to say about anybody, come sit next to me."
~Alice Roosevelt Longworth

There is something in business and life we never learn well enough —how to criticize and encourage those who rely on us for advice. It's more than a skill, it's an art. Because like other arts, criticism and praise are always imperfect; they contain within them both the affirmation of their need, and the possibility of their improvement.

Right now, there are people in your life whose work and behavior you are called on to evaluate, either regularly or from time to time. They may be immediate subordinates, clients, business associates, or competitors.

These people can make your future immensely richer, fuller, and happier; but it's equally true that they may hold your back or rise up against you. Much depends on how you treat them. Don't think for a moment that just because someone seems weak or powerless that you don't have to be concerned about him. It is the meek who will inherit your future, not only because they have a lot of pent-up energy; but also because you won't see them coming.

How do you get these guardians of your future to support your goals? How do you get them to believe in you? How do you get them to quickly and substantially develop the skills and talents you are looking for? How do you get them to make your life, your business and your day-today experience of working better?

The first and most important answer is this: don't pay attention to them.

Focusing your time and energy on getting them to like you or believe in you is counter productive. It sends the wrong message—that your business together is about you and them—and it distracts from what you should be doing, achieving your business goals.

FIRST, LAST AND ALWAYS YOUR BUSINESS SHOULD BE ABOUT BUSINESS

What is the important work you are trying to get done? What is the better or cheaper or more reliable product you are trying to create? Get your key people to set their eyes on that and you will teach them the most important lesson about work and job satisfaction: that the latter comes from paying attention to the former.

You will also, by way of example, be showing them how excellence looks. Your passion, your conviction, your belief in your business goals will inspire them.

They will see you coming in earlier than anyone else and leaving later and they will understand that you are doing so only because you want to create a better product.

That is the most important thing, but it is not enough. To get your business to take off and soar you need a team of superstars behind you. And to develop a team of superstars you must be prepared to praise them, criticize them, reward them and sometimes fire them.

I have spent many years fumbling around in this area. I've had some regretful failures but a surprising number of heart-warming successes. My method for training employees is part praise, part criticism, part honesty and part diplomacy. Ultimately it is common sense.

DON'T "OVERPRAISE"

To illustrate, let's take an example of something you shouldn't do. This is a mistake I've made more than once, and it's a common error among executives who are eager to develop good people. I call it the mistake of "overpraising." Let's say you have found a potential star performer—maybe your protégé. You are very pleased with his early performance. He's not quite there yet, but you want to make sure your praise is pure and positive. "Hey, kid," you say, "you're a genius." This has a very positive initial effect. He works even harder, and you keep telling him what a natural he is. You become a hero to him (temporarily), because you've recognized his talent. He becomes your savior, because you see in him everything that you want to see.

Gradually, though, something else happens that you didn't anticipate. Word gets out that he's a favorite of yours. This slightly damages everybody involved—him, you, and the envious. It's not a big issue, so you ignore it. He continues to do well, and his critics grow quiet. But along the way, he comes to the conclusion that maybe you were right, maybe he is a genius.

He becomes less likely to seek your counsel, less interested in other viewpoints.

He may even become somewhat temperamental and demanding. Eventually he becomes at least in your opinion—spoiled. From his point of view, you become a burden. The relationship may dwindle, even terminate.

Or something else happens: He goes cold and decides he is not a genius after all but a fraud. He loses confidence and gives up. This is bad for you and bad for him.

The mistake you made was in telling him he was a genius, or at least telling him too soon. By making the praise personal and not specific to the action (as in, "That report you wrote was a work of genius!") you make your relationship personal and not dependent on performance.

Personal preferences—publicly favoring one employee over another—spoils everyone involved. The praised employee becomes spoiled and feels entitled. The un-praised employee feels resentful. And you appear biased.

PRAISE THE ACTION, NOT THE PERSON

The bottom line is this: If you overpraise the person, you risk spoiling him and your relationship with him. If you praise the action, the person will get the idea that his future value is based on his actions, as it should be, rather than on his intrinsic worth.

In other words, he will realize that his value to the business is based on his performance, not his talents.

New Agers leadership gurus would disagree. They want you to tell your key people, "Your value resides in you, not in what you do. You are essentially good, and there is nothing you can do or say that will diminish that."

This is the kind of thinking that feels good but usually does more harm than it could ever do good.

As a general rule, it's much better to praise the action—the specific behavior. This says, "Your value resides in what you do. So long as you do well, you will be valued."

This message focuses your protégé's attention where it should be, on his actions and accomplishments.

It also acknowledges a very necessary truth: if he changes his behavior and does not continue to perform, he will become less valuable. Like it or not, this is a fact of life.

A colleague of mine recently discovered this wonderful and powerful idea from a TV program. (So, despite my long standing belief in the worthlessness of television, I guess you can sometimes benefit from watching it.)

In the show researchers studied two groups of children. The children in one group were told by parents and teachers how wonderful THEY were, while those in the other group were praised only for their good behavior.

As you've probably have already guessed, the first group—although it performed well—did not perform nearly as well as the second group. Moreover, the second group was better mannered and much less self-centered.

Remember these simple truths the next time you want to offer praise to a protégé or an employee.

SO WHEN IT COMES TIME TO LEVY CRITICISM, WHAT DO YOU DO?

The first and most important secret of effectively criticizing others is to forget about yourself. For example, if you criticize simply to give yourself some temporary relationship advantage, it will be apparent and resisted. If you criticize to demonstrate your superiority, it will be felt and rejected. If you criticize to exorcise some angry spirit inside of you, it will also be obvious and resented.

Criticize, when you do, only because you want to help. Any other motivation that may be inside you—showing your power, exercising your anger, displaying your knowledge—will defeat your purpose. It is much easier to have good judgment when you put yourself out of the picture. Then and only then, will you have a much better idea of what to say and when, because your thinking will not be clouded by self-interest. Moreover, your enthusiasm will show through, and the person you are helping will respond to that.

BEGIN WITH A SHOW OF FAITH

You need fertile soil in which to plant your ideas. Fertile soil is nourished soil, so always begin any relationship with a good ground foundation of praise. Before you make a single negative criticism, no matter how mild, find something positive—specific and positive—to say about the individual's behavior or performance.

It may not be easy. Especially with young workers who haven't got a clue, it is often difficult to find something about their early work that is praise worthy. Your first experience of their work will likely be negative. They will do something clumsy, or foolish or simply dumb. Resist the urge to tell them so, even if you would restrict your comments to their specific actions.

ASSIGN SMALL JOBS

Instead, give them a variety of smaller assignments until you can find something they do very well. (If you can't do that, then you have hired the wrong person.) When you do have evidence of a job well done, however small, praise them for it. Praise them publicly and then, if you can do so truthfully, tell them privately that you believe they can build on this little talent of theirs, that it can serve as a foundation on which to construct a very successful career.

People need to believe in themselves, and most importantly, they need to feel they have some natural strength or skill that can help them achieve. By identifying a specific praiseworthy behavior and connecting it with some possible inner quality, you create an idea that can fuel a lifetime of achievement. This, by the way, is not "overprasing" so long as it is truthful, specific act tied to performance.

ONCE YOU HAVE CREATED THIS FOUNDATION, YOU SHOULD FEEL FREE TO CRITICIZE.

I don't think it matters so much whether your criticism is harsh or mild, so long as it is heartfelt. Once your subordinate trusts you, once he believes that you believe in him, he will interpret your criticisms as he should—notations of where his work falls short of his capabilities.

So long as you are never dishonest or mean, and never criticize publicly, and always address your comments to the work, you should feel free to criticize. In the world of copywriting, I am known to be a fierce editor. It is not beyond me to write "gibberish" in the margin of a protégé's heartfelt writing. Recently, one of the most successful copywriters I know and himself a former protégé of mine, sent out a memo remarking on some harsh criticism I had leveled at a writer (and a friend) whom we had both been mentoring for some time. Here is what he had to say:

"Those comments really take me back. They are direct and right on the money. Now, I truly realize why I've had some success writing this stuff. I remember reading comments similar to these and they jolted . . . forced . . . embarrassed me into becoming a better writer. It's good, in a way, that he wrote such a terrible copy. Otherwise you wouldn't have responded as you did. And he would never have gotten the benefit of your frank criticism. A turning point in his copywriting career will be the next letter he writes. I now realize that's how I got better. There's no way I'd be here if you or anyone else had 'pussyfooted' around bad copy and tried to spare my feelings."

But here's the point of all of this. My earliest thought about the writer of that memo was that he was a natural-born copywriter, and I said so. Not just once, but many times over. This gave him the legs to stand when my criticism finally came.

HERE'S A 7-STEP FORMULA YOU CAN USE TO EFFECTIVELY DEVELOP A PROTÉGÉ OR A NEW EMPLOYEE:

1. Make him believe that you believe in him.

2. Work with him for a while. Give him helpful hints and gentle criticism. Expect some progress during this process, but not a lot. What you are really looking to do is establish the following:
   • Your authority, which you both need.
   • A common vocabulary so you don't confuse him.

3. After he's reached a plateau hit him with some direct, strong advice. But right before you make any comment, try to generate some good feelings about him. If you are harboring a bad feeling, it will come through. And there's usually no reason for a bad feeling if all you want is to effect a positive change.

4. Comment on the action or the issue, not on the person. If it is an idea or suggestion you are criticizing, make sure you fully understand the idea or suggestion before you criticize it. A good way to do this is to ask for clarification before commenting. Rather than say, "You are wrong about such and such," it is better to say, "Let me see if I have this right . . ." This approach often gives the person a chance to figure out for himself what was wrong with his idea. And that's exactly what you want him to do. Then you will not only have fixed the immediate problem in such a way that the individual "owns" the right answer, you will also have shown him how to review and criticize his next idea himself.

5. Don't ever be nasty in your criticism—but be honest. Although I'm not much of a believer in sandwiching criticism

between layers of praise—it seems so obvious and phony. But I must admit that when I do it, it works. I suppose the secret here is once again honesty.

6. Expect him to be hurt at first by your critical comments. If he responds defensively, don't fight with him. Remind him that you believe in him. Remind him that he has done good work in the past. Encourage him to keep at it. Tell him that he will succeed.

7. If he comes back later open-minded and eager to progress, you'll have made the leap you both needed. Progress should come pretty quickly after that point.

[KEY POINT]

Great leaders are perceived as powerful communicators because they listen more than they speak. When they do speak, they focus on the interests and concerns of the other person. They're also able to summarize and clearly present their case.

CHAPTER 16:
THREE COMMUNICATION SECRETS OF HIGHLY EFFECTIVE LEADERS

"If human beings don't keep exercising their lips, he thought, their mouths probably seize up. After a few months' consideration and observation, he abandoned this theory in favor of a new one. If they don't keep on exercising their lips, he thought, their brains start working."

~Douglas Adams, The Hitchhiker's Guide to the Galaxy[35]

If brevity is the soul of wit, taciturnity is the backbone of conversational power. How many times have you found yourself in a situation in which, not being entirely confident about the point you are making, you speak too long in supporting it? Each added statement sinks you deeper into the quicksand of your uncertainty.

SECRET #1: IN WRITING, AND IN SPEAKING TOO, SAYING LESS OFTEN SAYS MORE

Saying less saves you time. It keeps you out of trouble. And it gives

---

35 Adams, Douglas, *The Hitchhiker's Guide to the Galaxy*, Ballantine Books: September 27, 1995.
36 Greene, Robert, *48 Laws of Power*, Penguin: September 2000.

your words more force. In *48 Laws of Power*[36] Robert Greene put it this way: "Power is in many ways a game of appearances, and when you say less than necessary, you inevitably appear greater and more powerful than you are." This is the first and most important communication secret of great leaders

Louis XIV, a great leader, was a talkative young man. But when he became king, he reduced his formal conversation to the absolute minimum. In deciding matters of state the story goes, his practice was to hear both sides of all issues without commenting except to say, when all had been said, "I shall see." His subsequent decision was made without further discussion. This freed him from debates and gave the few comments he did make great power. One of his most famous statements was the quintessence of terseness: "L'etat, c'est moi." ("The state is me.")

Andy Warhol employed this strategy too. The king of pop art tried to avoid discussions of his own art. When he did talk about it, he made short, cryptic comments. By letting reporters and art critics interpret his minimalist statements, Warhol felt he got a better result than he would have gotten by articulating them himself.

A colleague of mine understands the protective power of taciturnity in vocal and in written communications. Busy with many other things, he frequently responds to long e-mail arguments with a single phrase like "Sounds good to me" or simply an enigmatic "Hmmm." While sometimes frustrating to those who want specific direction, it keeps him out of a lot of pointless squabbles and encourages his employees to solve problems for themselves.

I've had good success with my e-mail communications. However long my memo is when first written, I chop it down to less than a page—usually just seven or eight lines. It's amazing how much stronger they are. Not only do they have more power, they are more frequently read and more consistently replied to. Taking a little extra time to say less is an investment. Its dividends are substantial.

SECRET #2: LISTEN . . . AND WHEN YOU'RE DONE LISTENING, LISTEN SOME MORE

Skilled communicators not only say less when speaking and writing, but they also listen to others more. Dale Carnegie believed that *listening* well makes you appear a better conversationalist than does speaking well—and that it's certainly better than speaking too much. Carnegie told a good story about sitting next to an important businessman at dinner and saying nothing but "I see" and "aha" throughout the entire evening. The next day, he was shocked to hear that the businessman had praised him as a very bright young fellow and a charming speaker.

I've been listening to an audiotape program about listening. It makes the argument that you can increase your personal power by cultivating this often underappreciated skill.

The truth is I have mixed feelings about this concept. On the one hand, I know many accomplished people who don't listen well. On the other hand, I cannot deny the good sense of the argument. Skillful listening provides several irrefutable advantages, with it you'll become:

- A better negotiator
- A more effective manager
- A more charming leader
- A more successful salesman

A case in point: I had lunch one day with a very well known copywriter. He wanted to talk to me and my client collaborating on a few projects. We were very interested until he started speaking. He began by telling us all about us. I don't know where he got his information, but it was mostly wrong and/or outdated. Then he spent some time telling us what we needed, once again, without any apparent idea about our real needs. Finally, he pitched several ideas about how to solve problems we didn't have or address opportunities we had long ago taken advantage of.

He never asked us a single question or even looked at our faces to try to discern whether his monologue was hitting a chord. He simply talked. We came to the lunch 99% determined to do business with him. We left with the certain knowledge we wouldn't. The sad thing is that he will probably never know why. He certainly won't ask.

"Why," you may be asking, "didn't you stop him and correct his misunderstandings? Surely that would have redirected the conversation toward a more positive outcome."

ARE YOU A GREAT LISTENER?

Here's a clever way to find out: Ask someone who knows you. And listen to the answer. It's harder than you think!

Actually, we tried to subtly and carefully several times. But he treated our comments like digressions. He'd make some perfunctory statement and go back to what he was saying. He was so caught up in his own presentation that he ignored our thoughts.

We could have been more assertive, but with each new misstatement we became less interested in correcting him. It was becoming increasingly clear that he was not someone we'd enjoy working with. The reality, his weak communication habits and inability to listen cost him a new, profitable business venture.

But let's look on the flip side. Here's an example of good listening: I once negotiated the purchase of two very desirable oil paintings for myself and a client. The price quoted was $35,000. I had an argument ready—a good argument—for paying about $5,000 less. But instead of making it, I chose to listen. I said, "That price seems substantially too high. Tell me how you justify it." He gave me four reasons, two of which were solid and two of which were weak. I refuted the weak reasons with specifics. He was impressed, almost taken aback. He gave me a price of $29,500. I would have $32,000. Making my case after I had listened to his gave me an advantage, one that probably saved me a couple grand.

Although listening patiently may not come naturally to you—it didn't to me—the payoff can be big if you're willing to try and improve your skills. You can become a better listener simply by heeding 3 simple rules. Let's call them...

THE 3 GOLDEN RULES OF LISTENING

1. **Be quiet.** The first and most important rule is to shut up and let the other person talk first. Do that, and you'll be way ahead of the game.

2. **Listen on two levels.** First, listen to the literal content and next to the emotional story behind it.

3. **Summarize before you present your case.** Restating the speaker's thoughts and feelings ensures him that you understand him and makes him grateful and more open to your ideas. However, be very careful not to devalue the speaker's ideas or feelings with the words you choose to make that summary.

Frankly, I sometimes find it difficult to follow this advice. When I enter into a discussion, I have usually been thinking about it for some time, in detail, in depth and from various points of view. All this preparatory noodling gives me the feeling that I know exactly what needs to be done. As soon as the problem is brought up I want to provide the solution. That sometimes works. The difficulty is brought up. I give the solution. Presto . . . everyone is happy.

Just as often this approach backfires. I give my little speech only to discover there are other issues at stake, other details I wasn't aware of. So I am required to listen after all.

Sometimes having the solution hurts. People sometimes just need to be heard. They want to tell you their story, and they want you to listen to it. If it involves a problem and you think you have "the solution," you may be tempted to interrupt their story to offer it to them. This is usually a bad idea. Let them finish their sad tale and *then* ask if they have a solution. You may be surprised at how frequently they do. Why didn't they bother to tell it to you? It may be as simple as the need for sympathy. There's nothing wrong with that, so long as the need doesn't become neurotic. Constant comfort seekers are an unproductive, and draining. But when an otherwise good employee needs to vent, lend him your ears.

SECRET #3: FOCUS ON THE OTHER PERSON'S CONCERNS AND INTERESTS

Dale Carnegie found that being a good listener isn't the only skill that makes people think of you as a skilled communicator—it also has to do with WHAT you say when you finally do speak.

"People blunder through life trying to wig-wag other people into becoming interested in them," Carnegie said. "Of course, it doesn't work. People are not interested in you. They are interested in themselves—morning, noon, and after dinner."

A survey by a New York telephone company found information to back up Carnegie's theory. They made a detailed study of telephone conversations to find out which word was the most used. You guessed it: It was the personal pronoun "I." It was used 3,900 times in only 500 phone conversations.

And long before Dale Carnegie, Ben Franklin had this to say: "The wit of conversation consists more in finding it in others than showing a great deal yourself. He who goes out of your company pleased with his own facetiousness and ingenuity will sooner come into it again."

I learned this communication secret some years ago when I was working on my Ph.D. in English Literature at Catholic University. Hugh Kenner, a very prominent Ezra Pound scholar, had just finished a lecture. I walked up to the podium and asked him to autograph his latest book, a 10-pound tome on the controversial poet. I praised Mr. Kenner profusely and genuinely, as I was a big fan of his. The next day, the chairman of the English department pulled me aside and asked, "What did you say to Mr. Kenner yesterday? He was SO impressed with you! He predicted a great career for you in academia."

When you want to impress someone you're with, remember to focus the conversation, genuinely, on that person. Ask questions of the person you're talking to and express a genuine interest in them. Don't fake it, they'll be able to tell.

Remember these three communication secrets next time you want to impress someone or motivate an employee. They won't fail you.

Successful leaders are able to speak one on one, in small groups and in front of large groups. Their success is often attributed to knowledge and charisma, but the real reason is planning. They study their topic thoroughly and search for information their audience does not know. They present the facts passionately and stress one unifying idea. They always remember that they're speaking to individuals, even if there in a room filled with hundreds of people.

CHAPTER 17:
SPEAK MORE POWERFULLY . . .
LEADING BY PERSUASION

"Oratory is just like prostitution; you must have little tricks."
~Vittorio Emanuele Orlando

Speaking in groups—large and small—is an unavoidable requirement for those who wish to lead. In many ways leaderships is about persuasion—convincing people that your vision, your strategy, your solution is the one to follow.

Successful leaders develop the skills to persuade others in one-on-one situations, in small groups and in front of larger groups. No matter what size the audience you want people to listen, to understand and to remember what you're saying.

But that's often hard to do. According to one study I found in Newsweek, we retain, on average, less than one percent of the information we receive.

So how do you make your speeches unforgettable, and inspire the results you want?

HOW TO GIVE A GOOD SPEECH

In my experience there are only two strategies for making good speeches:

- You either talk spontaneously about what you know.
- You present a speech that you have carefully prepared before-hand.

In either case the secret to success lies in the fact that you are saying something *useful*. An expert will always have something useful and interesting to say about a subject. Decades of experience have rooted out all the bad and boring ideas from his head. What is left are ideas that work, that matter, that succeed.

If you don't have decades of experience then you need to do a lot of hard thinking, first-hand research and revising to come up with something useful. To make a really good speech (and an effective leader should attempt nothing less) you need to spend at least ten minutes in preparation for each minute of speech . . . if you don't you will probably disappoint both your audience and yourself. If you do, you will show yourself off as someone with good ideas, someone who can come up with solutions, someone to follow.

It's all about the preparation. As Muhammad Ali said about boxing, "The fight is won or lost far away from witnesses—behind the lines, in the gym, and out there on the road, long before I dance under those lights."

If you want your next speech to be a knock out, prepare yourself properly. Following are the best ideas I've learned about making good speeches.

TELL THEM SOMETHING HELPFUL

Let me say it again, this is the most important rule in speechmaking. What you say must benefit your listeners. Many novice speakers see the podium as a place to show how smart they are or to demonstrate their latest thinking. Nothing could be less interesting to an audience. Unless you are a guru of sorts—in which case you are not speaking to an audience but a fan club—your job is to help or enlighten your audience. They have taken the time (and in some cases spent money) to hear you. You owe them something valuable in return.

Before crafting your speech consider the audience—their beliefs, their feelings and their needs with respect to the speech topic. Ask yourself, how can I help them? Unless and until you make your speech about how to help your audience you will never be considered a great speaker.

TELL THEM SOMETHING THEY DON'T ALREADY KNOW

The most common criticism of speeches is, "He said nothing I don't already know." It's not enough to give your audience useful information, then. At least some of it has to be new to them. How do you know what's new and what's not? You don't. But if you prepare your speech properly, if you spend ten times your speech time thinking and reading and conducting interviews, you will surely come up with ideas, facts and perspectives that will be new to some of your audience some of the time.

My favorite trick for coming up with new and different ideas is this. Read what others have said on the same subject with a contrary point of view. Think: "In what way is this idea wrong or specious or shallow?" Most of the best ideas I've had over the years have come from this simple tactic.

A speech doesn't have to be 90% new to be effective. In fact, any speech that approached even 30% to 40% new stuff would be incomprehensible. A good rule of thumb is 80% what they know expressed from a new perspective and 20% of what they probably don't know expressed as simply as possible.

UNIFY YOUR SPEECH WITH A SINGLE, OVERARCHING IDEA

The less you know about something the more complicated it

seems. As you acquire knowledge and experience of a given subject matter you begin to see patterns. Things that seemed confusing and unrelated before you now see as associated, sometimes even one of a kind.

If you speak about what you know and spend a good deal of time preparing your speech you will begin to see how certain ideas and elements of your speech are related. Use these observations to come up with an overall theme for your speech. What is the overriding idea here? If I had to summarize my message in 12 words or less, what would it be?

It's not easy to come up with a single theme for every speech, but if you do so you'll make your speech much stronger. A unifying theme makes all the ideas, facts and perspectives of your speech easier to understand. And by designing your speech around a single theme you'll find it easier to edit out all the fluff. Most importantly, a single, strong idea will resonate in the minds of your audience. It will, eventually, persuade them.

FOLLOW THE "THREE TELL 'EM" RULE

Very early in your presentation, if not in the opening line, you must tell the audience what you are going to speak about. Make it clear, concise and useful. Remind them of this primary idea at least once more during the course of the speech and then once again at the end. This is probably the oldest rule in speechmaking and it is for a good reason. It works. It makes it easier for your listeners to follow the details and easier for you to stick to the point.

LET THE AUDIENCE SEE HOW MUCH YOU CARE ABOUT YOUR IDEAS

If you care about your big message—and you should—then you will have a natural enthusiasm for talking about it. This is perhaps your greatest asset as a speaker. Let that spirit show. It will ignite interest in everyone who listens to you. Don't fake enthusiasm. Be authentic. If you find that you aren't charged about your speech, then keep working on it till you are.

STICK TO WHAT YOU KNOW IS ABSOLUTELY TRUE

The only way you can feel sure of your big idea is if it is an idea with which you've had experience. If, for example, you were talking about the best way to hire new employees then be sure your big idea is something you personally discovered from hiring employees—some interesting little trick you employ (dropping your pen to see if they pick it up) or some larger observation you've made (that, for example, testing doesn't work). If you do so it will ring true. If your big idea is something you've read about but have no personal experience of, watch out. You are setting yourself up for trouble.

CHANGE DIRECTIONS FREQUENTLY

When structuring your presentation take into account a survey in *Business Week*. According to the magazine, the typical U.S. executive has an on-the-job attention span of six minutes. So, to accommodate today's channel-surfing attention span, think of your presentation as six-minute TV scenes. If you are using audiovisual aids, make sure each one has its own headline. And always plant a verbal flag in each scene. For example a statement such as "Let me highlight this idea for you." This signals the main idea of that particular six-minute scene and grabs attention. Also, always vary your audio/visual techniques and move around a lot. Most importantly remember to have fun and your audience will too.

CREATE "THE PERFECT MOMENT"

One goal of your presentation should be to create what Spalding Gray calls "the perfect moment". That's the moment in a speech when your big idea is suddenly made to seem powerful, correct and even

**8 COMMON SPEECHMAKING "RULES"
YOU *SHOULDN'T* PAY ATTENTION TO**

I found the following 8 "rules" in a popular book on speechmaking. It occurred to me that they are all wrong.

1. **Don't be nervous.** What good does this advice do? Telling some- one not to be nervous is like telling someone not to flinch when you slap him.
2. **Use a podium.** This is a big mistake. Using a podium will only make your presentation appear static and boring.
3. **State your objective.** You need to tell them what you are going to tell them, yes, but the objective is not your objective, it's their need. Tell them, in other words, how your speech will help, instruct or enlighten them. Make it clear that they will benefit from what you have to say.
4. **Speak slowly.** Speed doesn't matter. People talk at an average rate of only about 120 words per minute, but the brain can absorb the meaning of words when spoken at 480 words per minute. What matters in speech is articulation, not speed. Pace your speech with your enthusiasm. Pronounce each word. Be natural.

brilliant. There are all sorts of ways to do this. The way I like to do it is with metaphor. After I've introduced my idea and shown how it works and provided data to support it I find some fun way to present it in the form of a metaphor. How is my big idea on hiring like, for example, pitching in the World Series? How is it like singing the blues?

By going at the big idea from different directions—metaphors, allegories, quotations, etc.—you can often achieve that sense of, "Yes! I get it. That's right!"

SPEAK TO INDIVIDUALS, NOT THE ENTIRE GROUP

Listening to a speaker is a one-on-one experience. Speaking to your listeners should be also. Speak your first sentence as you are

5. Tell a joke to get started. Too risky. If you feel you need to tell a joke to loosen yourself up chances are you won't tell it well. It's safer and just as effective to lead with a strong, compelling statement or question.

6. Cover all bases. I've never been able to cover even half the bases. If you research your speech subject properly, if you do some serious thinking, if you prepare yourself by seeking ideas and talking to other people, you'll have much, much more to say than you will be able to say in the time allotted you. Decide beforehand: what are the most important issues and address them. Leave the lesser matters to the Q&A period, if there is one.

7. Summarize at the end. Never summarize. Summary is always boring because it is, by definition, abstract or diluted. Rather than summarize restate your big idea in a different way. Make your last line a knock out punch.

8. Keep control at all times. Like the "don't get nervous" advice, this one isn't helpful. The way to keep control is not to think about control. Think about what you are saying. Think, "I have something important to tell these people. They really need to hear it." Focus on your ideas, not yourself.

looking at a particular person. It might be someone you know or just someone who seems friendly. Make eye contact. Smile. Try to get a reaction. Then move on to someone else and try again for a reaction. You should build rapport with an audience one person at a time. Ron Hoff, in *I Can See You Naked*[37], says you should act like a dog that's glad to see you, has no pretenses and knows exactly who he is.

MEMORIZE THE FIRST AND LAST LINES OF YOUR PRESENTATION, BUT NOTHING ELSE

The speaker who reads his speech is sure to fail. He can't make eye contact. He can't become passionate in any genuine way. He can't

---

37 Hoff, Ron, *I Can See You Naked*, Andrews McMeel Publishing: October 1992.

light up his audience. You need a strong first sentence or three. (These are the lines that you are giving to individuals, with eye contact and a smile.) And you need a strong closing line so your audience knows when to applaud, but in between you need to speak strongly from the heart.

In preparing your presentations, therefore, don't use scripts, just note cards. What you write on your index cards or visual aids should be no more than simple reminders. The idea is to jot down a short phrase that will remind you of a story or an idea about which you can speak confidently. Ron Hoff recommends using your index cards as a "memory map" that allows you to go where you have to go without relying on a linear text.

- Jot down the basic points you want to cover.
- Visualize those points graphically. Make little cartoons, sketches, and stick figures to illustrate them.
- Create a pathway, like a game board, and pepper it with these little illustrations.
- Think Candyland. Make it simple. Don't fuss with it. Your memory map is there to stimulate your thinking, not substitute for it.

LAST IS BEST, FIRST IS OKAY TOO

When you are going to make a presentation or even give an interview, try to be the last one seen. Studies show, and my experience confirms, that the people who do the best in multiple interviews are those who come first or last, regardless of how good they actually are. The next best position, in terms of recognition and appreciation, is the first spot.

If you are scheduled for an interview or sales presentation and are put in the middle of the pack, consider asking for either the earliest or latest slot. They just might accommodate you.

JUST BEFORE YOU SPEAK...

Take a little walk to get the blood pumping and clear your head.

FOOL PROOF YOUR PRESENTATION

Here's a checklist for any presentation you have to give in a hotel or any other new place:

- Make sure the chandelier in the middle of the ballroom doesn't overhang your screen.
- Before you start, turn on your slide projector and test for bobbing heads.
- Be absolutely certain the local Boy Scout group isn't going to have a bugle concert in the room next door.
- Get the feel of your room at least two hours before your presentation.
- Make sure any presentation boards can be seen from the entire room.
- Decide where you will place your timepiece.
- Critical: Make sure you have the extension number of the hotel A/V specialist.
- Check the lighting system. Make sure you understand how it works.
- Watch out for cords that snake along the carpet. Have them taped.
- If you are using a lavaliere mike, make sure you know where the hot spots in the room are.
- If you have bar service before your presentation, make sure it gets shut down before you begin speaking.
- Expect things to get lost unless you keep your eye on them.
- Trust no one.

(Excerpted from *I Can See You Naked* by Ron Hoff[38])

Then check yourself in the mirror—you don't want shaving cream in your ear.

Next, ask yourself what the main idea of your presentation is and promise you will make that clear to your audience.

And right before you 'take the stage' say a few words to someone to make sure your vocal chords are working properly.

38 Hoff, Ron, *I Can See You Naked*, Andrews McMeel Publishing: October 1992

Lastly, take a few deep breaths and smile—it only hurts for a second.

STRENGTHEN YOUR SPEAKING VOICE

If you speak a lot, you might want to develop a stronger speaking voice by taping yourself and analyzing what you hear. Is this a voice you'd want to listen to? Describe the voice you hear and make three resolutions for improvement. Use them and future tapings to monitor your voice as you practice and improve.

Most people don't like speaking publicly. But the more you do it, the better you'll become and the less anxiety you'll feel prior to making your presentation. In addition to following the ideas above, the best thing you can do to improve your skills is to practice. If you need a real life arena why not volunteer to speak in your area of interest during a local chamber of commerce meeting? You can also volunteer to speak at events hosted by any organization or association you may belong to. If you don't belong to any you're missing out on a great opportunity to boost your speaking skills and network—it's time to sign up!

Successful leaders know when they should negotiate and when they shouldn't. They use strong negotiating skills including the ability to find common ground as well as uncover value-creating differences. They're able to avoid biases and partisan perceptions, keep a level head if tempers flair, and remain positive.

CHAPTER 18:

HOW TO BE A SUCCESSFUL NEGOTIATOR: HANDLING OBJECTIONS AND OBSTACLES LIKE A PRO

"In all negotiations of difficulty, a man may not look to sow and reap at once; but must prepare business, and so ripen it by degrees."
~Francis Bacon

If you want to be a complete leader you need the persuasive skills to inspire belief and enthusiasm. But even when you are very good at getting people to buy into your vision you will have occasions when the more pragmatic skills of negotiating will be necessary.

Successful leaders need strong negotiating skills for times like these. They need to be able to structure arguments, amass supportive data, state positions clearly, deflect criticism and communicate advantages even under the most difficult of conditions.

The first skill of a good negotiator is to know when to do so. Most of the deals I've made in my career have required little or no negotiating. I know what I want out of the arrangement. I find out what the others want by asking. Then I think about how everyone can have

155

what he wants and usually I come up with an answer.

Once you have an answer that appeals to the parties involved you have the basis for a good and sustainable deal. But getting to that point often requires a good deal of thought and study, usually to the point of detail. Marc Diener, the author of *Deal Power*, calls this becoming "fluent with the details of your deals." [39]

You have to know the issue inside and out if you're going to present a persuasive argument for your side. This includes knowing how your "deal is unique" and positioning these special characteristics to your advantage.

Richard Shell, a Wharton professor and author of *Bargaining for Advantage*[40], makes the case that successful negotiation is 10% technique and 90% attitude. Wharton says that you don't have to sell your soul to get what you want. He says that good negotiating is a mix of competition and cooperation.

I couldn't agree more . . . the great negotiators I know are those who take a broader approach to setting up and solving the right problem. Great negotiators can see the big picture.

They envision the most promising architecture and take action to bring it into being. These negotiators are game-changing entrepreneurs.

They have a keen sense of the potential value to be created and understand how to get it.

For most people these skills are not natural. The good news is that every one of them can be learned.

It may help to think of negotiation as a skill of three parts. That's how *Harvard Business Review* writer James Sebenius puts it.

1. Issues are on the table for explicit agreement.
2. Positions exist. (Where the negotiating parties stand on the issues.)
3. Interests are the underlying concerns that would be affected by the resolution.

---

39 Diener, Marc, *Deal Power: 6 Foolproof Steps To Making Deals of Any Size*, Henry Holt & Company, Inc.; January 1998.
40 Shell, Richard G. *Bargaining For Advantage: Negotiating Strategies For Reasonable People*, Penguin USA Reissue edition: June 5, 2000.

There are many different techniques to negotiation, some good, some bad. Below are the ones that have helped me most when I've had to negotiate. I think they'll help you too.

10 SIMPLE STEPS TO NEGOTIATION SUCCESS

Step 1: Assess All Interests

Focus on the full set of interests of all parties, rather than fixating on price and positions. To do this, you must learn as much as possible about the other party. This is very important. You need to get a feel for who you'll be dealing with. For example, if you're going to be negotiating with a business, pick up company brochures, the latest news and trade journal clips that have been written about the company. And if it's a person, experts suggest asking questions of those who have dealt with them before.

And most importantly in this step you must try to find common ground—the deeper issues that both you and the other party will agree on. Those issues should be the basis for the beginning of your negotiations.

Step 2: Set Your "Bottom-Line" Goal

Determine what you have to walk away with . . . your "bottom-line goal" as an article in *Nation's Business*[42] magazine called it. Pick the one thing you want to leave the negotiation with. Ask yourself, if you had to have only one thing, what would it be? Make that thing your "bottom-line goal." Do enough thinking here to make sure this goal is realistic and attainable.

Step 3: Search For Value-Creating Differences

Look beyond common ground for value-creating differences. What's unique about your position? What's unique about the position of the other side? Think about how you can use these differences to your advantage and make your position more valuable to the both of you.

---

42 Pouliot, Janice S. "Eight Steps to Success In Negotiating," Nation's Business, April, 1999.

Step 4: Ask Yourself 'What's The Worst That Could Happen?'

Determine your worst case scenario. One very useful technique for solving problems and negotiating differences is called BATNA—an acronym for "best alternative to a negotiated agreement." The phrase was coined years ago by Roger Fisher, Bill Ury, and Bruce Patton in their book *Getting to Yes: Negotiating Agreement Without Giving In.*[43]

The basic idea of BATNA is to contemplate the worst case scenario, the worst possible outcome, *before* you engage in a negotiation. In essence you simply face the fact that you might not reach any agreement at all. You think about it and accept it. Then you figure out what the best alternative to a negotiated agreement would be. The idea being, if you are unable to compromise and reach an agreement, you won't be stumped. For example, your best alternative might involve approaching another buyer, or enduring a stalemate, or even going to court. If you have a BATNA, it will allow you to negotiate strongly without feeling anxious if things aren't moving forward well. You already know the worst that could happen.

Step 5: Make Sure You've Met The Person

Don't let your first-ever meeting be at the bargaining table. If you don't know the person or people you'll be negotiating with, try to set up an initial meeting for no other reason than to get acquainted. This will take some of the pressure off. It's most important when there's a lot at stake for the negotiation. Paul Fox, president of Fox Performance Training—a company that specializes in negotiation training for managers—uses this technique. He says it works best if you're up front and simply tell the other party you'd like to have a pre-meeting to get to know one another.[44]

Step 6: Set An Agenda

Create a negotiating agenda. This should be an outline of the issues that are going to be discussed and how you're going to make the discussion happen. The agenda is a way of making sure the negotiations

---

43   Fisher , Roger, Ury, Bill, Patton, Bruce. *Getting To Yes: Negotiating Agreement Without Giving In*, Penguin USA; 2nd edition: December 1991.
44   Pouliot, Janice S. "Eight Steps to Success In Negotiating," *Nation's Business*, April, 1999.

stay on course and unrelated issues aren't brought in. Like mediation specialist Linda Stamato says, this kind of plan should be flexible and agreed upon by both parties.[45] I don't think this is necessary in every negotiation, but again, if there's a lot riding on the outcome an agenda can certainly help.

Step 7: Watch Out For Biases

Avoid role biases and partisan perceptions. One of the main roadblocks to successful negotiation is bias. It comes as no surprise that most of those involved in any type of negotiation have a built-in bias toward focusing on their own positions. Harvard Business Review writer James Sebenius says despite the clear advantages of trying to reconcile deeper interests, most negotiating parties have a hardwired assumption that their interests are incompatible. My gain is your loss type of thinking. Research in psychology supports this false view as the norm. In fact, during 32 studies of 5,000 subjects negotiating over money, participants failed to realize compatible issues half the time.

In most situations however, there *is* common ground. There are deeper issues all parties will agree on, it's just a matter of finding them. Again, you need to work to find these issues and they should be the basis of your negotiation.

Step 8: Control Your Temper

Keep a level head when tempers flair. Lashing out during any negotiation is a big mistake, even if the other party started it. It's too easy to create enemies in business. You will do so even if you try not to. But in the long run, you'll have much greater success—and you'll enjoy your success more—if you don't have dozens of people out there in the marketplace hoping for (and possibly planning for or abetting) your demise.

If your negotiations start to get heated the best thing to do is to remain polite. Listen. Make it clear you can be trusted. Then acknowledge the other side's point of view. Try if you can to obtain smaller, less important agreements. These techniques are proven to work in the most volatile situations in fact many of them are used daily by the

---

45 Pouliot, Janice S. "Eight Steps to Success In Negotiating," *Nation's Business*, April, 1999.

ASSESS YOUR NEGOTIATING SKILLS

Think about the last time you were involved in a negotiation. It could have been for something as important as a pay raise or as simple as convincing your significant other to go to a certain movie. How well did you do? Now pick apart the negotiation. What could you have done differently? Better? Identify your weak areas and work to strengthen those skills—practice them. Make a plan for future negotiations using the 10 Steps outlined in this chapter.

New York Police Department's hostage negotiation team.

And by all means never, ever get personal. Even if you can damage the other party, never make any threats. They'll just come back to haunt you in the end, and you'll have made an enemy you would have been better off without. Case in point, I recently suggested to a colleague that she make an offer to buy a company I know.

What should have been a very pleasant opportunity for both of us turned into a fight. It happened because she made a fundamental, but very common, negotiating mistake:

She introduced the stick with the carrot and any productive negotiation went out the window.

So, even if you do have a threat in your pocket, don't take it out and wave it around. Chances are the other person is aware of it anyway. You'll do much better by making the positive case, even if it costs you a little more in the short term.

Step 9: Learn How To Deal With A Stalemate

If there's a stalemate, find the underlying cause. In my experience, a stalemate occurs because of bias.

It's because all of the parties involved are focusing on some small issue and have lost sight of their common interests . . . the reason for the negotiation to begin with.

This is why it's so important to keep your eye on the big picture when you're negotiating.

Step 10: Know How To Handle A Deadlock

When you're deadlocked, buy some time. If you find yourself in a deadlock, it's best to take a break. Walk away for awhile and clear your head. But before you do, set a time to return to the negotiating table. It could be that same day or even later that week.

If you can do nothing else during your next negotiation, I recommend following the advice from a reporter who attended a Harvard Business School seminar on handling difficult business negotiations: Erase "but" from your vocabulary. For example, instead of saying "I understand how you feel, but we can't afford to pay you a hundred grand," say "I understand how you feel, and we can afford to pay you $65,000."

CHAPTER 19:
STANDING UP TO BUSINESS BULLIES THE RIGHT WAY

"No one can make you feel inferior without your consent."
~Eleanor Roosevelt

Sooner or later, we all end up working with a bully—someone who tries to achieve his career goals by browbeating subordinates, intimidating colleagues and trying to topple his bosses. Bullies don't play fair. They find ways, situations and techniques that give themselves extra power and they use that power to dominate.

Bullies are bad for business because they are not focused on business. Their interest is themselves. But if bullies are bad for business, they are worse for the people they deal with. They can make you do things you wouldn't do for or with anyone else. They usually pressure you into decisions you don't feel good about, don't enjoy enacting, and—almost always regret later.

THE BULLY AND THE PUSHER

This leads to an important distinction between a bully and a pusher. A pusher is someone who does everything he can to get you to do things you might not want to do, but both of you know you should do. When and if the pusher pushes you into doing such things, you feel good about yourself and grateful to him. A pusher however annoying has the business's best interests at heart. So long as your interests are aligned with your business (and they should be) you have nothing to fear from a pusher.

> 4 out of every 5 employees—that's 23 million people—will face a business bully in their career. (Study by Wayne State University)[46]

It's a miserable experience to work with a bully. And it's often very difficult to get yourself free of him. An *Early To Rise* reader, in a posting in "Speak Out", the Early To Rise chatroom, says, "You've got to watch for the warning signs of a bully and break off the relationship early. Thomas Jefferson once said that the art of living is learning to recognize situations that will lead to trouble and avoid them."

So true, but it isn't always easy to avoid the bully. For one thing, you may not be in charge of the relationship. It may be something that is forced on you. The bully might be your boss, or a consultant, or even a fellow worker who happens to sit next to you. You might think you could stop dealing with a bully the moment you figured out his game. But the typical bully doesn't let you do that. He has a bag filled with emotional tricks he uses to keep you in his orbit.

Another reason it's not always easy to break free of bullies right away—they don't usually start off by bullying you. The secret power of the bully is his charm. If he were only pushy and obnoxious, he would never work his way into your psyche. But he doesn't start out that way. He begins his relationships with wit and humor, compassion and intelligence, promise and benefit. He makes you like him and then tries to make you dependent on his reactions. You start to care about offending him. You dread having to argue with him. That said, you should make every effort to identify bullies as soon as possible and get yourself free of them as soon thereafter as you possibly can. One thing about a bullying relationship that's almost always true: it gets worse as time passes.

---

46 Chabria, Anita, "Do You Work For A Bully Boss?" *The Industry Standard,* March 12, 2001.

ARE YOU BEING PUSHED AROUND BY A BUSINESS BULLY? ANSWER 4 QUESTIONS TO FIND OUT...

1. Do you feel harmed physically or emotionally by the behavior of a coworker or boss?
2. Do you feel demeaned or humiliated at work on a regular basis?
3. Are you yelled out, lied to or subjected to other behavior that you find questionable?
4. Do you have coworkers or a boss who you've seen bullying others currently or in the past?

If you answered 'yes' to any of the above questions, you have a business bully in your life. Act quickly to get rid of them![47]

HOW TO AVOID A BULLY

My wife is great at avoiding bullies and other negative types. The moment she comes in contact with someone who tries to push her around, she makes quick work of him. She usually makes a joking comment that lets him know, in no uncertain terms, that she doesn't see the world the way he does. And after that, she ignores him. She ignores him to the point of rudeness when he speaks to her and then desists from any further interaction. She won't return phone calls or answer email. She will barely acknowledge him in person. She stays polite, but she doesn't engage.

Engagement is just what the bully wants. Having the sense that he can overpower you in some way, he does everything he can to lure you into the ring.

When I encounter a bully, I try to follow my wife's example. And often I am successful. But sometimes I find myself pulled into the ring. Sometimes it's because I am suckered by what the bully offers—the benefits of working with him. Sometimes I am challenged by the idea of overcoming him. Whatever my motivation, the experience is always unpleasant. And I always end up regretting it.

---

47   Chabria, Anita, "Do You Work For A Bully Boss?" *The Industry Standard*, March 12, 2001.

You can keep bullies from messing up your business and you life by following 5 suggestions.

1. Start by admitting to yourself and a trusted friend that you are being bullied. Say the words out loud. Say, "I am letting so-and-so bully me." This will give you some immediate relief. It will remove the added pressure of having to rationalize your unbalanced relationship with someone who clearly doesn't have your best interests at heart.

2. Next, set a time limit for liberating yourself. It could be a week, a month, or three months, depending on how entangled your relationship is.

3. Set intermediate goals and write them down in your monthly, weekly, and even daily to-do lists. Give yourself specific objectives, such as "Today I will respond to his taunts by saying, 'Jack, I don't think that is a fair comment.'"

4. Free yourself bit by bit. If you try to force too much too soon, you will probably get yourself into an emotional situation that is over your head. Gradually, the bully will notice that the relationship is changing. He will sense the power moving back to you. He may try to resist it, try to seduce you one more time—try almost everything as he gets desperate.

5. Hold strong.

When you're faced with a bully, focus on accomplishing one small objective at a time. Before you know it, you will be in the catbird seat. And you'll feel like a brand-new, newly powerful person.

Great leaders understand that when you ask a question you give up a little power. To ask questions without giving up too much power, leaders assess and acknowledge the ladders of power—learning what they can ask, when they can ask it and from whom they should or shouldn't approach.

CHAPTER 20:
ASKING QUESTIONS LIKE A BORN LEADER

"A fool can ask more questions in a minute than a wise man can answer in an hour."
~American proverb

Many more times than once, driving lost in an unfamiliar neighborhood, my wife has given me the good advice to stop and ask directions. I have seldom been able to do so. "I can find my way," I insist. Twenty minutes later I am forced to admit defeat and do what I should have done in the first place.

Professional comedians have made much of this common male fear. And well they should. Most of the men I know are as adamant about finding their own way as I am. And most of the women I know can't understand why.

For me, the reason I don't like asking directions is because it makes me feel submissive. And I don't like to feel submissive, because I live in a world where submitting is a disadvantage. When you submit, you relinquish power. And power in a competitive, hierarchical world, is wealth. This is important to understand if you wish to succeed in business. Asking questions, though useful in the short term, can be damaging to your long term success.

I realize this is both an unpopular and a politically incorrect perspective. But it's true. To understand why this is so, I need you to indulge me in some further admittedly unsophisticated observations.

THE WORLD OF BUSINESS IS A WORLD OF POWER

Those who have more powerful resources—financial, intellectual, and emotional, etc.—generally accomplish more than those with less. In the traditional women's world of home and children, sharing is the preeminent skill. (For a great analysis of this see almost any of Deborah Tannen's books.)

If you want to succeed in business you can't ignore how the game of power is played. Getting ahead in this world is not about beating up everyone you compete with. Rather, it's more a question of giving each man his due. Most men want as much power as they can get. However, they realize that to get power they need to share it. When two men meet, they often have a "feel out" discussion in which they find out, in a seemingly casual way, certain important things about each other.

Primarily, they are interested in discovering areas of dominance, not to contest them but to accede to them. Like boxers in the first round, men will verbally jab and shift during a preliminary conversation, moving this way and that, feinting and parrying, trying to discover who is the better businessman, moneymaker, athlete, intellect, talker, comedian, etc. The questions will be so casual, almost to the point of being banal, that the average female auditor might think nothing is being communicated at all. In fact, in what amounts to just a smattering of conversation by most women's standards, men extract a great deal of vital information. At the same time they come to some sort of psychological agreement as to where, on Power's Ladder, each of them stands.

THE LADDER OF POWER

There is not just one ladder of power. There are dozens, if not hundreds, of them. And for every relationship men quickly figure out, and more importantly, tacitly agree to relative positions on all of these many ladders.

"He can talk better than I can, but I can kick his ass if I have to. He has more money than I do, but my girlfriend is better looking than his wife. He is a stronger negotiator than I am, but I am more cunning." And so on.

But the interesting thing is, as I suggested above, that the other man is having this sort of conversation with himself.

"He is physically superior to me, but I can outtalk him. He is able to attract better-looking women than me (Damn It!), but I can flash my bucks." And so on.

Men calculate these internal rankings, more or less consciously, all of the time whether they admit it or not. Doing so is a necessary outcome of living in a competitive, hierarchical world. Men understand, almost from the moment they meet someone, who will have the upper hand in what area.

By assessing and acknowledging relative positions on the many different ladders of power, men can quickly find a relationship that works cooperatively. This is an essential skill in business because success in business is just as much about cooperation as about competition.

Women may not easily recognize this game of power and politics. They may not see its relationship to posing questions in the workplace simply because of the differences in the way they perceive asking questions.

But the cold hard truth is this: asking questions at work can hinder your future—especially if you are trying to carve out a niche as a skillful leader.

You must realize that each time you ask a question you give a little bit of power away. And if you ask enough questions, you will eventually give up not only your power but also your competitive rank. To ask questions without realizing this is to put yourself in an unnecessarily weak position from the start. (Granted, this is not always true in all situations. There are questions that do not yield power, and those should become apparent.)

Put simply, you must remember this: You can only hurt your position if you ask the wrong person the wrong question. It comes down to where you are on the power ladder and who you are asking. Every good leader must be able to make this assessment. Once you understand the principle that the asker gives up a little power in exchange for the answer, and you've learned about the power ladder in your environment, you will know when to ask questions, whom to ask, how to phrase them and when to figure out the answers on your own.

WHEN TO ASK

You can feel free to ask questions about matters that are clearly outside of your area of competence. If, for example, you are known to be a strong marketer you can ask all the questions you want about product quality, customer service or technology.

You can ask questions about your forte when you are seeking to instruct or gather opinions. If you are discussing a project with your key employees, you can call for opinions without losing any power so long as you reserve the final decision . . . or at least the sanctioning of the final decision . . . to yourself.

WHOM TO ASK

Ask questions of your superiors when you believe they have your best interests at heart– which is to say, the best interests of the business at heart. Always ask good questions of your superiors—carefully thought out, specific and concise questions. You don't want to waste their time. And you don't want to appear foolish.

Ask questions of a mentor you can trust. The mentor relationship is trustworthy, because it is based on recognizing that the mentor has the power now but will gradually cede it to the protégé in return for hard work and loyalty. Asking questions makes you seem likeable. Subordinate, but likeable. So don't be afraid to ask questions of a mentor.

Ask your subordinates questions when their specific knowledge or experience will help you reach a solution. In *The Leader of The Future*, Stephen M. Bornstein, the CEO of ESPN, and Anthony F.

Smith, an international business consultant, say good leaders feel comfortable asking "thoughtful" and "guided" questions of their followers.[48] They must avoid the appearance of a "know-it-all" leader. They must admit when they don't know something, and admit when they make mistakes.

You can ask anyone outside your power center (the business environment in which you seek to have power) any questions you want. This would include friends, family, colleagues and consultants. Questions posed outside your power center can't affect your power. But if you ask anyone too many questions, even your closest friends, you will show yourself as uncertain and therefore a little weak. They won't tell you that. In fact they'll deny it vehemently if you ask them. But their view of you as a successful and powerful person will be diminished.

HOW TO ASK

When you ask questions speak with confidence. Make your sentences short and to the point. When you receive an answer ask only as many follow-up questions as needed to understand. Don't debate the answers.

Be thankful for the answers but not effusive. Keep in mind that the suggestions that may seem brilliant one day may seem impractical or even absurd the next. Resist the urge to discuss your worries. You are a business person in search of ideas, not a neurotic in need of psychological counseling.

WHEN AND WHOM NOT TO ASK

Don't ask questions of someone more powerful than you if you have reason to believe they don't like you. They will see your asking as a form of subservience and will use that against you.

Don't ask questions to make people feel good. If you want to make

---

48 *The Leader of the Future*, The Drucker Foundation, New York: 1996.

a particular employee feel smart or talented or valuable, do so by providing specific compliments about his behavior. Don't create a phony
counseling situation when you aren't honestly in search of counsel.

Don't ask questions to ingratiate yourself with anyone, ever.

If business were a cocktail party you could—and should—be able
to ask any question that you like. But since the world of commerce is
a world of power, an intricate maze of adjustments and seizures and
give-and-take, you have to be as shrewd about asking questions as you
are about anything else.

When it comes to business, in other words, act like a man (even if
you're a woman). Treat questions as dangerous, even if it means that
sometimes you have to drive an extra few blocks in an unfamiliar
neighborhood.

PART FOUR

LEADING THE TROOPS DAY BY DAY

CHAPTER 21:

IMPROVING ALL OF *YOUR* RELATIONSHIPS:

HOW TO GET PEOPLE TO LIKE YOU AND DO WHAT YOU WANT

"You can be totally rational with a machine. But if you work with people, sometimes logic often has to take a backseat to understanding."
~Akio Morita

If you want to become an effective leader, you're going to have to build strong relationships. It's not important for everyone to like you, but it helps if they do. At the very least, it's important for them to have a positive impression of you in business.

To accomplish this, you must learn how to relate to people positively, even the ones you don't like. (Whether you realize it or not, you may need their help some day.) And don't worry, no matter how you've behaved in the past it's never too late to begin generating positive feelings. It's true. You can quickly take charge of how you are perceived in both your business and personal relationships by modifying your behavior in just the slightest of ways. It all comes down to basic psychology . . .

FIRST IMPRESSIONS COUNT

According to Nicholas Boothman, author of *How to Make People Like You In 90 Seconds Or Less*, what you do in the first few minutes of every personal encounter determines how people will respond to you later on. First impressions do count, Boothman believes, more than most people realize.[49]

I agree. And it's not just the very first impression. It's the first impression you give each and every time you greet someone. Each and every time you encounter a friend, family member, or business associate, do the following:

1. Be aware of how you feel. Make yourself feel positive and allow that feeling to be reflected in the way you hold yourself.
2. Make eye contact: Always look the other person directly in the eye, even if only for a moment.
3. Beam. Be the first to smile. Let your smile, as well as your body, show that you're happy to see him/her.
4. Make your "Hi!" or "Hello!" sound friendly.
5. Take the lead: Extend your hand first.
6. Shake his/her hand strongly. Shake it like you mean it. Remember, your handshake provides an instant message about you. Are you an important person? A friendly person? Someone who can be trusted? Answers to these questions (and more) can be conveyed by your handshake. So ask a few trusted friends or colleagues to interpret your handshake for you. Make sure the signals you are giving are those you intend. If they aren't, make changes.
7. Lean toward him/her: An almost imperceptible forward tilt will very subtly indicate your interest in and openness to the other person.

However much you can, know what you want out of every new relationship or new encounter *before* you begin it. This will allow you

---

49 Boothman, Nicholas *How to Make People Like You In 90 Seconds Or Less*, Workman Publishing Company; (September 18, 2000)

6 WAYS TO MAKE PEOPLE LIKE YOU EVEN MORE

One of the most powerful personal-development experiences you can have comes from Dale Carnegie. In his How to Win Friends and Influence People program, Carnegie says you must do the following 6 things to get people to like you.

1. Be genuinely interested in them.
2. Smile.
3. Remember that a person's name to that person, is the sweetest sound in any language.
4. Be a good listener and encourage them to talk about themselves.
5. Talk in terms of their interests.
6. Make them feel important and do it sincerely.

to channel that positive first impression into something meaningful and beneficial.

SMILING: THE MOST IMPORTANT OPENING TECHNIQUE YOU'VE GOT

It's key to smile when you meet someone for the first time or for the 101st time. This is because when you smile it gets the other person to smile, and that opens many doors. I learned the 'smiling technique' from a colleague, who uses it successfully every time he wants something from me.

I am not sure he does it intentionally or that he even knows he does it. But I suspect he learned it during his twenty-year career as a successful salesman.

It's quite simple really. Almost every time we meet he makes me smile. I have observed that every time he pops his head into my office, he carries a big smile. He says something with the purpose of getting me to smile back. And it works. This is not an easy accomplishment. I can sometimes be a temperamental bastard. But even in my foulest moods, my colleague has an astonishing record of squeezing that meltdown smile out of me.

What's his secret? That's what I'd like to know. But I do know this, it starts with the fact that he tries. When someone cares enough about your feelings to try to make them improve, it feels good.

You may be the sort of person for whom this comes easily. If so, you need only realize what a talent you have and resolve to use it more. If you are less-than-gifted in the sunshine department (charisma-challenged, like me), you should consider adding this technique to your persuasion arsenal.

If it doesn't come naturally, you'll have to practice. Hint: You have to be really good to make someone else smile when you are frowning. So start off by smiling yourself. If you are really retarded in this area, you might want to practice in the mirror before you experiment on a live subject.

When you start to use this technique you'll quickly find it will not only make you feel good, but it will give you a sense of power. Most importantly, your smiling subject will be more open to your ideas and interests.

And don't forget to smile while you're on the telephone, the person on the other end can tell. And it works in the exact same way.

MAKE EMOTIONAL CONTACT

To make a positive, powerful impression on people you work with, make an emotional contact with them. It is much easier to be persuasive with someone if he thinks you like him and have his interests at heart.

The most effective way to convey this is to look him in the eye and—while you have his momentary attention—think caring thoughts about him. Think, for example, "I know you don't mean to act like an S.O.B. I like you." This will stimulate positive feelings in both of you.

If you are shy about looking at someone directly, try this: Challenge yourself to identify the color of your "target's" eyes and reacquaint yourself with that color every time you talk to him. This will get the dreaded eye-lock accomplished. Then all that's needed is one positive thought.

You can do it. Give it a try.

AVOID DALE CARNEGIE'S 3 C'S THAT CAN DESTROY ANY RELATIONSHIP

Dale Carnegie also points out three habits that can diminish and even destroy relationships. All three, happily, begin with the letter C making them easy to remember. If you want a good relationship here are three things you must NOT do:

- Criticize
- Complain
- Condemn

As someone who loves to moan and groan, I have enormous difficulty with this advice. But it's never failed to work wonders for me. If you have a problem relationship, business or personal, this advice will have a profoundly positive effect on it. By the time things go bad, there is so much direct or indirect criticism going on that the relationship itself gets stuck. And unless you make a conscious effort to stop being negative, things won't get better. There's just too much negative stuff you hardly even notice you are doing. This formula is very strong. Even if you do nothing else but this, you'll ensure trouble-free relationships.

I feel the need to make an important clarification here. I recognize that from time to time we are asked for criticism or that it is our duty to criticize. I'm not suggesting you discontinue this. But if you avoid the impulsive criticisms, the careful, necessary ones will be better received and have a much better effect.

To develop this skill begin by trying to spend the next day without criticizing anyone, complaining about anything, or condemning any person, place, or thing—not even slightly. It won't be easy, but do it anyway—24 hours straight. And then, if that works, pick out someone with whom you're having a bit of trouble. Make yourself a promise not to criticize, condemn, or complain about him for a full week. If that works, extend it to a month. In a month's time, you'll have a whole new, very positive relationship with that person. Guaranteed.

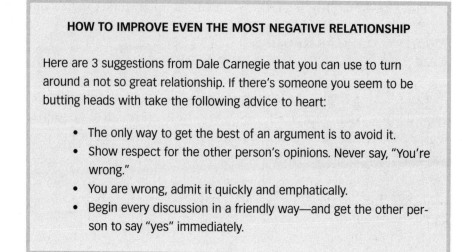

HOW TO IMPROVE EVEN THE MOST NEGATIVE RELATIONSHIP

Here are 3 suggestions from Dale Carnegie that you can use to turn around a not so great relationship. If there's someone you seem to be butting heads with take the following advice to heart:

- The only way to get the best of an argument is to avoid it.
- Show respect for the other person's opinions. Never say, "You're wrong."
- You are wrong, admit it quickly and emphatically.
- Begin every discussion in a friendly way—and get the other person to say "yes" immediately.

And this is important too: When someone criticizes you, respond by first saying "Thank you." Even if you go on to refute every word of what was said, letting the critic know you appreciate the comment will go a long way toward making your defensive conversation successful.

DON'T FALL VICTIM TO OFFICE GOSSIP

What is more fun than hearing about the misfortunes or misdeeds of a fellow worker? Does life in the office offer any sweeter revenge than seeing a nasty boss or surly subordinate get his comeuppance? None—and that is a memory you can (and will) carry with you forever.

Office gossip is like junk food: You can pretend you don't like it, you can even publicly denounce it, still you know you can't completely resist it.

But try. Like so many things in life, office gossip is a temporary indulgence with long-lasting, undesirable side effects. For one thing, it damages team spirit. This is no small cost if you are a leader and are concerned with and compensated by team productivity. For another thing, it demeans your stature. Even your co-conspirators will think less of you for doing what they themselves know they shouldn't do. If you consider the kinds of activities you can engage in at work, this falls into the lowest category. It's not only unproductive, it's destructive.

Make yourself this promise today: Gradually you will indulge less in this bad habit. Start by desisting from gossiping yourself. The next step is to maintain a neutral position when someone brings it to you. The ultimate step is to be able to discretely change the subject without seeming like a wet blanket. If you find you're having trouble watching your tongue, try this: The next time someone attempts to get you to join him in badmouthing a colleague or employee, imagine that your comments are being broadcast to the entire company on a speaker system. Speak as closely to the truth as you can, but try not to say anything that you wouldn't say in front of everybody.

If you begin doing just some of the things you learned above on a daily basis you'll immediately notice an improvement in the way others perceive you. And as a leader, this could not only make your job easier, but make you feel more confident and better about yourself.

Leaders understand that empowering their employees with new skills works to their advantage, and to that of the company. But they don't focus on teaching employees themselves. They put into place internal mentoring and orientation systems so their best employees train the others.

CHAPTER 22:
CREATING STELLAR EMPLOYEES WITH 5 TRAINING TIPS

"Teaching isn't one-tenth as effective as training."
~Horace Mann

According to a study of 1,600 businesses, companies that spend the most money training their employees can promote internal candidates almost a third of the time, compared to only one fifth of the time for companies that spend less than half as much on their training.

Is that good? And is it scientific? Could it be that companies that are employee-oriented enough to spend more on training are also more likely to promote their employees over outside candidates? I believe in training, but most of what I've seen is bad. A good training program does at least three things:

1. It teaches skills that dovetail with your business's needs.
2. It motivates and inspires as it teaches.
3. It challenges employees to put their new skills to work immediately.

There's only one way to ensure that the training programs you pay for meet these three standards: You have to check them out for your-self or have someone you trust do so.

I also believe training must be selectively given. Keep in mind that even good training works differently with different kinds of employ-ees. In my experience, training programs work best with superstar employees. The irony in this is if your best employees don't get train-ing from you, they'll seek it out and get it on their own—and they'll probably pay for it too! In other words, the most effective training you can provide will be mostly unnecessary for the people whom it will benefit the most. And on the other hand, training your bad employ-ees is useless. Their goal is to do as little work as possible. At the office, this means they spend a lot of their time reading magazines, playing computer games, and daydreaming. Send them to a seminar and you'll be lucky if they show up at all.

There is a naïve impulse to try to "save" a poor or rebellious person by providing him with more benefits. (The same impulse that makes you *think* you can appease your enemies by kowtowing to them.) One cor-porate version of this tendency would be to send out weak employees for training—as you might send out a dirty shirt for laundering. Guess what? The stain that bad employees bear is almost always permanent.

SUPERSTAR EMPLOYEES VS. THE LAGGARDS

So how do you define a superstar—someone capable of doing a job you'd describe as excellent? It's not easy. But one way to do it is in the negative—by identifying the characteristics of non-superstars.

- comes to work on time
- leaves work on time
- makes personal calls at work
- promises to do more than he does
- blames his boss/job/mother for his failures
- spends more than a minute chatting about personal things
- thinks about his personal life at work
- doesn't really care how a project turns out if it's not being done his way

- misses deadlines—even if only by a little
- is late for appointments
- does things just because someone asks him to
- is bored
- is uninterested
- is tired/blue/worried/depressed

Anyone that fits into the above category you should try to avoid training if at all possible.

TRAINING: WHO, WHAT, WHEN AND WHERE

My first and most important training recommendation is to:

- Give all of your best people almost unlimited access to training.
- Deny it (however you can) to the laggards.
- Provide it selectively to the group in the middle.

You might be able to accomplish the third part of my recommendation by making any seminars you provide desirable and exclusive. This is training tip number 2. For example, when you announce a program, advertise its benefits. Tell your employees how they will personally benefit from attending. Tell them too, how the business will profit. Consider limiting the number of attendees. Also a possibility: some sort of application process. Finally, let it be known that all employees who take training are expected to indicate afterward what they thought of the training, what they got from it, and most importantly, how they will put what they learned to good use.

Training tip #3: always include training in your budget. And plan training into your work schedules and business strategies. Every business is different, but every growing business should be able to spend some number of dollars on training for every type of employee it can benefit.

However, if you're spending a lot of time training and retraining your employees, you may be making a big mistake. You can change things for the better by passing on the responsibility for teaching new employees to your students. Here's how: Let's say you are a marketing manager and you have had to teach your assistants how to purchase printing, make up list grids, or use a marketing spreadsheet. Rather than continuing to teach each new employee the same routine (how boring!), train the next one that you hire not only the routine but also how to teach it. It's training tip #4 and it works . . .

By training your student how to teach a skill, you force him to learn it extremely well (well enough to teach it without embarrassment) and you free yourself from future repetitious efforts. Training someone to teach takes time. It also takes some skill. You have to consider not only the tasks that are involved in the job but also the best ways of explaining them. Still, it will be well worth the time and effort that you put into it. There are additional benefits to establishing this kind of mentoring program:

- You provide the new employee with a corporate friend, someone to turn to for advice.
- The mentor feels responsible for the new employee's performance—and they both learn that responsibility is best when shared.
- For a while at least, a separate pair of eyes will be carefully reviewing the early work of every new employee. This should result in fewer mistakes—fewer problems that will need to be fixed later.
- The mentor will probably rise to a higher level of commitment and dedication to the business. He'll take himself and his job more seriously.

For my money, a decentralized mentor system is generally superior to a centralized training facility. Sometimes, you need both. But whatever you do, don't keep teaching the same old thing yourself.

ORIENTING NEW EMPLOYEES

One way to orient new employees is to provide them with a copy of a very interesting and useful book called *What the CEO Wants You to Know*.[50] In it, Harvard MBA Ram Charan breaks down business to its basics, using his own family's small shoe store for examples. To Charan, running an international corporation is similar, in the most important aspects, to running a small retail store. He says that everyone in business has to focus on four things:

1. Cash generation: Is more money coming in or going out?
2. Return on assets: How much money is the business earning as a percentage of the assets it owns?
3. Growth: Is your business getting bigger or smaller?
4. Customers: Are they happy or not?

In addition you can have your CEO or chairman write a short manual to supplement *What the CEO Wants You to Know* titled "What I'd Like You to Know About Our business." This is training tip #5. Here is where you can explain to your new employees, in simple terms, your company's "mission." It's also where you can identify the values and characteristics that spell success in your company. And where you can list the numbers Bob Reiss, a columnist for Inc. magazine and a former CEO, says are essential to every business. Generally, he says, there are only four numbers every CEO, CFO, and owner must know. He says they amount to "numeracy"—numerical literacy. They are:

1. His company's cash flow
2. The cost breakdown of his products
3. The break-even analysis for his company
4. The break-even analysis for each of his products

Once your employees understand that business is concerned with these questions and numbers, they will be much more likely to do the right thing—without your even asking them to.

---

50 Charan, Ram *What the CEO Wants You to Know: How Your Company Really Works*, Crown Business; 1st edition (February 13, 2001)

Contrary to popular belief, businesses are hierarchical and don't rely on teamwork. Leaders understand this. They treat each employee with equal respect but they have different expectations for each one. Teamwork has its place, but it's only effective in situations where something specific needs to be done in a certain amount of time.

CHAPTER 23:
TRANSFORM YOUR TEAM INTO A WINNING ONE

"A team should be an extension of the coach's personality. My teams were arrogant and obnoxious."
~Al McGuire (former basketball coach)

There has been much written in recent years about teamwork in business. The general drift of the advice goes something like this: "You and your employees are a team. In a team, everyone is equally important. The secret to making a team—and in this case a business—work is to treat everyone equally, for everyone's contribution is essential.

I believe that leading a successful business involves teamwork, but I don't think the aforementioned idea is a very good one. For example in Dick Lyles' book *Winning Ways: 4 Secrets For Getting Results By Working Well With People*, a Ken Blanchard parable on success, Albert is hampered in business by his inability to work as a team member. His supervisor tells him to visit a local college football coach for advice. What he gets are four rules[51]:

---

51 Lyles, Dick *Winning Ways: 4 Secrets For Getting Results By Working Well With People* Berkley Pub Group; 1st edition (December 4, 2001)

1. Make people feel stronger rather than weaker.
2. Team-built projects are better than those built by individuals.
3. Avoid right/wrong absolutist thinking.
4. Focus on building toward the future, not complaining about the past.

Like most self-help stuff on the market these days, Winning Ways has a dash of good insight, a cup of common sense, and a pot full of tepid water. Lyles and many other business writers view business as a kind of egalitarian sporting event where all contributions to the team are equally valued and equally rewarded. In such a world, it makes good sense to treat all suggestions as good, all ideas as sound, and all efforts as valuable. To run a team in this sort of world, Lyles' leader would give everybody, every suggestion, and every interest all the support possible. He would make every team member feel good and make every team effort a pleasant one.

In the real world, this is exactly what you don't want to do.

THE AWFUL TRUTH ABOUT TEAMWORK

In the competitive world of private enterprise, businesses strive to grow and prosper—not by treating all their workers the same but by recognizing that they are almost all different. Some will contribute more than others, some will work harder than others, some will come up with lots of good ideas, and others will hardly ever think of anything but the next coffee break.

Successful business leaders—and successful coaches, too—treat all their team members with equal respect but have different expectations for each one. The expectations (and the responsibilities that derive from them) are based on individual performance, not on ideological beliefs.

A basketball coach, for example, will ask the guy who has an 88% free-throw average to shoot penalty shots—not the guy who drops only half the balls in the bucket.

Great business leaders search out among their employees those who can do more, think better, work harder, and care more deeply—

and assign those individuals different and more significant levels of responsibility. In other words, making a team—or a business—work is not about believing blindly in equality. It's about recognizing and taking advantage of inequality.

BUSINESSES ARE HIERARCHICAL... NOT BUILT ON A TEAM MENTALITY

The primary business organization is hierarchical. One man on top, several men under him, several men under each of those, and so on. There is a reason for this. Businesses are complicated affairs. You need lots of experience to run one properly. You also need experience to develop a profit instinct—and a profit instinct is absolutely critical to the success of any business. The hierarchical organization puts a priority on experience because its main goal is to achieve an objective not reach a consensus. It does so by placing authority where it belongs—with those who have experience, with those who have proven themselves.

Great business leaders run their companies mostly through a chain of command. When they lead teams, they run them the way good coaches run their teams—by treating everyone with equal amounts of respect and by pushing everyone to contribute as much as they are capable of contributing to the cause.

WHEN TEAMS WORK

The team concept is useful for business, but only in *certain situations.* For example, having a group of employees work together as a team is very effective when you need to get something specific done by a particular time and you need the cooperation of a group of people to do so. But, even then, you will do better if the team has a strong leader who is the undisputed top dog—the man who has ultimate power and whose experience, judgment, and motivations must be trusted. This person has to be a strong leader who will push and guide everyone to get the job done.

The kind of team I like is one that has four to seven players and one coach . . .

The coach is the boss, the undisputed top dog. On my team, loyalty and compliance are highly valued traits. On my team, there is a wrong way and a right way to do things. And as far as Dick Lyles' four rules about teamwork are concerned, I'd revise them as follows.

1. Make weaker people stronger and stronger people weaker when and as it suits the general good of the business.
2. Recognize that good products/projects require the input of many people, but that only one person with one vision should have the final say.
3. Consider all sides of any important question but when you come to a decision about what to do, make it definitive. Black and white is easy for everyone to understand. Gray is not.
4. Analyze mistakes carefully—and publicly—to understand and communicate what went wrong. Try not to embarrass the mistake makers, but don't make the avoidance of embarrassment your top priority.

Ultimately, progress is made by the combination of one strong leader and several talented followers. When you are in the position of following, do so loyally and helpfully. When you are asked to lead, do so without hesitation and focus on the objective rather than on yourself or your team.

CHAPTER 24:

HOW TO MAKE MEETINGS WORK THE WAY *YOU* WANT THEM TO

"I am a great believer, if you have a meeting, in knowing where you want to come out before you start. Excuse me if that doesn't sound very democratic."
~Nelson Rockefeller

Whether you have three people or 30,000 working for you, your job is to inspire them to follow your vision. A prime time to do this is at meetings, large or small, private or public. It's not easy to motivate people at meetings. Nobody likes meetings. They are often seen as disruptive, disorienting, even useless. Unless you run the meeting right, it is likely to end up as a net negative, with your people confused, distracted or disturbed.

As I said, business meetings aren't limited to conferences in the boardroom, informal lunch meetings are just as important.

Every time you get together with your employees and/or colleagues to discuss business you have a chance to advance your business and moneymaking goals. Like it or not, every business meeting and every social meeting with a business colleague, is a forced performance. You are on stage. The person or people you are meeting with are the audience. What you do, how you act, what you say, your gestures, and the tone of voice you choose, is making an impression. It can be good, bad, or indifferent. It might improve your image, tarnish it, or reinforce an existing prejudice. You can't ignore this fact, so why not take advantage of it by committing yourself to making each meeting a successful one?

ACHIEVE RESULTS WITH PREPARATION

Every time you have a scheduled meeting you should create a plan. Your plan should include a specific personal goal, for example "I will leave the meeting with an agreement from Jeff on the new product." It should also include ideas about how to attain that goal like "I'll make him a quick, logical argument—and if he doesn't go for that, I'll remind him of the favor he owes me."

But when you're running a meeting, you have to do that and something more: You have to make sure the meeting provides an opportunity for everyone else to benefit. Planning a meeting with only your own goals in mind can result in failure, especially if those who attend fail to plan too.

The best way to make sure you have everything in order for a successful meeting is to follow 16 simple steps. These are the procedures I use to plan all of my meetings and they have never failed me:

1. **Decide if you really need to meet at all.** First before you call a meeting, ask yourself if the same work might be better handled by phone/e-mail/memos, etc.
2. **Determine what you want from the meeting.** If you decide to hold a meeting, spend a few minutes thinking about what you want to get from it. Figure out the objectives. Ask yourself, "What is my goal?" and "What goals should attendees establish for themselves?" If there is not a particular objective simply resolve to improve the relationship or improve your image as a smart and capable person.
3. **Set a reasonable goal for the meeting.** If you want to

close a deal but realize it can't be done at this particular meeting, settle for something else, such as an agreement on one part of the deal "if and when" it comes to fruition. If your goal is to improve the other person's impression of you and you know he thinks you are a scoundrel, don't press too hard. Be happy with showing him that you are perhaps not all that bad. You want your goal to be achievable, of course, because if it's not you're going to push too hard and damage a potentially good relationship.

4. **Translate any objectives or goals into benefits.** Ask yourself "Why will achieving the goals be good?" This is important because to accomplish any objective specific or general, you need to figure out how it is going to benefit the person or persons you will be meeting with. Formulate an "if ... then" approach. If the person you are speaking to agrees to help you with your objective, then he will enjoy certain positive results. A word of caution here, if you can't figure out beforehand what such positive results would be, your objective may be unreasonable and you should reconsider.

5. **When you schedule a meeting, make sure all the attendees know what its purpose is beforehand.** Also, it's important to meet with no more than seven people at a time. If you think you need more than that, you may need to have two or more meetings or reorganize your business.

6. **Always set and maintain a reasonable time limit for every meeting.** Most meetings are much longer than they need to be. Set a shorter time limit than you think you need and press people to finish on time. If you do, they probably will.

7. **At the beginning of the meeting, restate the goals and benefits you've determined.** Make the meeting's purpose specific and limited. In group meetings it's often a good idea to let someone else, the next-most-senior person in the room, state the purpose and objectives of the meeting. This will give you a chance to find out if you are on the same basic track. It may also provide an opportunity to get a feeling for where everyone is, roughly speaking, on the issue at

hand. Then, ask whether there are any objectives that need to be added to the agenda before you go any further.

8. **The meeting should be broken up into at least two parts.** During the first part, the problem or opportunity should be presented and commented upon. This is also when you would present your "if . . . then" proposition if one exists. If it does, be sure to present it subtly. In most cases you won't want to put it as directly as "If you do this for me, I'll do this for you" because it will make the other person feel manipulated. (That said, make your point and keep making it until you've achieved your goal. If you make this a habit, you'll be amazed at how much you'll get done and how powerful you'll feel.)

9. **The first part of the meeting must be as "open" as possible.** Try to limit the number of objections that arise during this period—including your own. One way to help this process is to suggest that all objections be handled later on. In the second part of the meeting, all problems and implementation should be dealt with.

10. **In the beginning, ask only open-ended questions.** These are questions that can't be answered with a "yes" or "no".

11. **Be prepared to react like a leader.** When people ask for your opinion as they inevitably will if they've been trained to follow your lead, turn the question around toward them saying "What do YOU think about it?"

12. **Make a mental note of anyone who hasn't said anything.** After others have chimed in, ask his opinion.

13. **If you can't engineer a sensible plan of action from the group, put one together yourself.** But talk about it as if it had come from them. In fact, much of it should have come from them.

14. **Put everything in writing.** Ask the next-most-senior person to create a written action plan with specific deadlines and identified responsible executives on the spot.

15. **Every single encounter is an opportunity.** Remember to consider every meeting as a chance to better your career.

Besides contributing to the group objective, is there a way to use the meeting to promote your own position? Many times, the best way to serve yourself is to serve the group. Prepare well. Come with good ideas. Impress everyone. Get your agenda accepted. Demonstrate to those attending that you will play a helpful and important role in solving the problem or achieving the goal.

16. **Remember your objectives and those of others.** Before closing the meeting, make sure everyone has had an opportunity to work toward his objective. Then close the meeting on an upbeat note.

If you approach your meetings with this kind of goal oriented plan, you will rarely if ever be disappointed.

SO HOW COME SO MANY BUSINESS MEETINGS DO FAIL?

A recent article in the Harvard Business Review took a closer look at why so many corporate meetings fail to achieve a future goal. Ram Charan, a former business professor at Harvard, a consultant to "top executives," and the author of *What the CEO Wants You to Know: How Your Company Really Works,* said the problem is with the meeting itself.[52] What looks like general agreement on a specific game plan is, in truth, "silent lies and a lack of closure," leading to a culture of "indecision" and "false decisions."

Charan says a successful meeting begins with dialogue, and I agree. He says business leaders who want to make sure that good decisions get made and are then implemented must create a dialogue that has four characteristics:

1. Openness: The outcome should not be predetermined. I believe an easy way to prevent this is to not hog the podium. Make sure everyone invited feels free to speak.

---

52 Charan, Ram *What the CEO Wants You to Know: How Your Company Really Works,* Crown Business; 1st edition (February 13, 2001)

2. Candor: There should be a willingness to discuss the unpleasant things, to air the conflicts. The fastest way to ruin candor
   is to criticize. If someone says something wrong, silly or naïve,
   don't ever criticize. Simply rephrase his comment and ask him
   if that is what he meant. More times than not he will realize
   what he's done and correct himself unilaterally. Don't ever
   attack or criticize the group either.

3. Informality: Formal, prepackaged presentations stifle candor.
   To maintain an informal atmosphere make it clear that you
   will take the time to address serious objections raised.
   Remember, this should happen in the second part of the
   meeting. And be aware of the dominate people in the group.
   Don't allow them to speak too much. If there's someone who
   hasn't said anything ask that person a question to get them
   involved.

4. Closure: At the end of the meeting, everyone should know
   exactly what he is expected to do. One way to be certain of
   this is to make sure the meeting ends with at least one specific and positive plan of action. This plan should always coincide
   with your objectives.

It is easy to embrace the idea of open dialogue, but it is much more
difficult to make it happen. If you have tried it yourself, you know
what I'm talking about. There is too much time wasted listening to
comments that are simply uninformed, naïve, narrow-minded, or just
plain silly. Still, you should try. Someone who has the dialogue
approach down to a science is Jack Welch of General Electric. Welch
has instituted three "social operating mechanisms" that encourage
useful dialogues:

1. The Corporate Executive Council (CEC): The company's top
   leaders meet four times a year for 2 1/2 days to share their best
   business practices, assess the current market, and identify the
   company's most promising opportunities.

2. The Session C Meeting: Once a year, Welch and GE's senior
   VP meet with the head of each business unit and his top per-
   sonnel manager. They talk about leadership and organization-

al issues and how to identify the best talent.

3. The S-1 Meeting: This is a yearly meeting held about a month after the Session C Meeting. Welch, his chief financial officer, and members of the office of the CEO meet individually with each unit head and his or her team. They discuss strategy for the next three years.

4. The S-2 Meeting: This is another once-a-year meeting similar to the S-1 Meeting, but it focuses on a shorter-term horizon, usually 12-24 months.

The whole process is unrelenting in terms of demanding that divisional leaders involve their managers effectively in the decision-making process. And demanding the creation of dialogues that are open, candid, and informal, that result in specific action plans.

There is no question in my mind that the executive who runs his meetings this way will achieve more and suffer fewer setbacks than the employer who is all output and no input. That said, it must be acknowledged that quite often the senior leader is the senior leader precisely because he has a better understanding of how the business works and a more aggressive attachment to its primary goals.

BUT SOMETIMES MEETING SUCCESS IS A MATTER OF NUMBERS.

Malcolm Gladwell, in *The Tipping Point: How Little Things Can Make A Big Difference,* observes that there are numerical limits to what the ordinary mind can do.[53] So if our ability to process information and make decisions is limited numerically, it makes sense that there should be some corresponding limit to the number of people we can effectively deal with. I've suggested some of those limits for meetings and some of the reasons I believe they matter.

For brainstorming: I believe three is the perfect number for generating breakthrough ideas. You need two smart people who know the market and think of themselves as idea makers. Plus another smart

---

53 Gladwell, Malcolm *The Tipping Point: How Little Things Can Make A Big Difference* Back Bay Books; (January 7, 2002)

person whose opinion the idea makers respect. It is also possible to brainstorm with three idea makers. The important thing is understanding the dynamic. At any point in time, two of the idea makers will usually be talking in a dialectic (building an idea by challenging each other) while the third person listens attentively as the audience. This tension between performers and the audience brings out the best in everyone. Of course, the roles can shift fluidly. You can put more people than three around a table at your next brainstorming session, but it will not improve the outcome. If anything, it will dampen the mood.

For round-table meetings: Gladwell's rule here is "no more than eight." And in my experience, it is a very good rule. Put two dozen people in one room, and you'll get nothing but "less" out of a round-table meeting. Less legroom, less energy, less creativity, and less satisfaction. So resist the temptation to be "inclusive." Touchy-feely temptations are almost always best avoided. You know that.

For classroom-style seminars: The limit for a classroom-style seminar seems to be 25 to 35, depending on how dynamic the speaker is. If you put 40 or more in a room, the teacher will lose control because he won't be able to zero in on individuals.

For lecture-style seminars: There doesn't seem to be a limit to the audience for a lecture-style seminar. It appears to depend on the power of the speaker. I know some good speakers who are compelling with 50 people but lose their touch when the crowd gets larger. I have done a reasonable job with groups as large as several hundred. But the real pros, like Tony Robbins, can keep thousands enthralled.

For managing your department or business: Five is the best number. Six or seven is manageable. Eight is possible. If you have more than eight people reporting directly to you, you are in trouble. If you think you have everything under control, you have more problems than you know. The whole trick of good management is to keep this level of management small. You do that by subordinating one group inside another and either firing or demoting the weaker manager.

For a working group: I don't know what the M.B.A.'s call it, but I use the term "working group" to signify the number of people you can effectively control. My rule here is "one level squared." In other words, the number of your direct-line subordinates times the number of direct-line subordinates you allow each one of them. If you run a very tight ship, that could be 25 (5 x 5). Or it could go up to 64 (8 x 8)—but that would definitely be stretching it.

For a division: In *The Tipping Point: How Little Things Can Make A Big Difference*, Malcolm Gladwell observes there is a great deal of historical and anthropological evidence to suggest that human beings cannot effectively congregate in groups much larger than 150 people.[54] He cites numerous records of tribal groups, exploration teams, military outfits, and so on. All of these groups have naturally limited their own growth to that number. I don't know why that should be, but it certainly is an interesting thought that there's a natural, human limit for any working division, just as there is for a working group.

Regardless of the meeting setting or size you should always remember to sell the big idea. James O'Rourke, director of the Fanning Center for Business Communication at Notre Dame says selling a big idea starts off by clarifying it and setting the goals or objectives outlined above.

O'Rourke says you also must "link" your objectives to those people you wish to inspire, and the way to do that is to break your vision down to specific objectives that are "measurable, observable, and rewardable." I believe this is noteworthy advice. I believe people will work harder to achieve the objectives set during your meetings if and only if you can create a work environment in which their efforts are noted and rewarded.

---

54 Gladwell, Malcolm *The Tipping Point: How Little Things Can Make A Big Difference* Back Bay Books; (January 7, 2002)

CHAPTER 25:

THE BEST WAY TO DELIVER BAD NEWS: WHEN TO WRITE ... WHEN TO PHONE ... WHEN TO HAVE LUNCH

"Surely human affairs would be far happier if the power in men to be silent were the same as that to speak."
~Benedict Spinoza (1632-1677)

Someone once told me that you should always deliver bad news in person. I didn't think much of it at the time, but over the years I've come to appreciate what an important rule of business it is. In fact, now that we are all fully entrenched in the world of e-mail, it is a rule that has become more important than ever.

Do you know someone like this? Very nice to chat with, reasonable and fair ... but you hesitate to open his e-mail or read his memos because they are sometimes nasty, derogatory, and condescending? I've known several people like that. One was a very talented marketing executive who was charming and self-effacing in person—and Attila the Hun-ess on paper. At least a dozen employees walked out on her because of the "suggestions" she made in her memos.

Another, a brilliant and insightful consultant, was given to vicious attacks on colleagues and even clients. For no apparent reason and at no predictable moment, he would send out a virulent message. It was as if he had a writer's version of Tourette's syndrome.

Yet another executive I work with is extremely good and protective with his staff but combative and condescending in his e-mail communications with his colleagues. To make matters worse, he almost never ventures out of his offices, which means he is admired and liked by his staff, and isolated and disliked by his colleagues. This has caused him considerable harm in terms of lost deals, joint ventures, etc.

I AM FOREVER STICKING MY PEN IN MY MOUTH

As an editor, I have made the mistake of memorializing my criticisms way too often. After an hour with unruly copy, I fall into a kind of evil mood during which each new textual weakness becomes a personal affront—something that begs for retaliation. Before very long, I'm thinking, "What do you take me for, a doormat for drivel?" And then the red ink starts flowing—like blood. Would I act this way if the writer were sitting before me, in the flesh? I hardly think so.

And don't think this is a problem only for grumpy old men. It affects everyone, even someone as nice and charming as you! Just yesterday, for example, I reviewed a reply to a proposal. The letter, written by one of the nicest executives I know, began by saying something like "We have only one concern about your suggestion that . . ." and then went on to explain, very clearly, why the proposition would "never be acceptable" and how it "failed to recognize a key element of our business" . . . and so on.

It was clear to me, having the advantage of perspective that this intentionally benign letter was going to offend the recipient. He was going to read it, or that portion of it, as intractable and self-aggrandizing. Worse, he was going to see in this very nice executive a new, bad side of her personality that he wouldn't like and would react to later.

It was a small, unintentional error. She was merely trying to state her point clearly, so there would be no misunderstanding later and no unnecessary discussion. But the opposite would have happened. There would have been memos back and forth—the deal getting more fragile with each one—and then sore feelings later on. This is not an isolated incident.

E-MAIL AND RETURN BUTTONS MAKE IT WORSE

And now that we are all speaking to one another by e-mail, it is happening every single day.

I did it again. I copied a "sensitive" e-mail to the wrong person. It's soooo embarrassing. In what I thought was a confidential memo to my partners I characterized someone's proposition as "insane." I neglected to check the "recipient" box before I sent it off - and as fate would have it, he got it.

There's an old bit of business advice that goes something like: "Always speak about everyone as if he were in your presence." I've never been much good at following this rule. I enjoy slander - but I have gradually come to realize that it is not a good business practice.

An amazingly high percentage of the calumnies I utter find their way back to the victims. It's never a pretty situation, and when you say nasty things in print it's worse, because it's permanent. And with e-mail, it's worst of all, because it is so easy to broadcast the recrimination yourself . . . and it happens so fast! I'm sure you are better mannered than I. Still, it won't hurt to consider the following e-mail rules.

1. Never write anything about anyone in an e-mail message you would not want that person to hear about.
2. When you simply can't resist a witty barb, don't use any button that allows you to send the message automatically to a group of people unless it is absolutely necessary.
3. Double-check the recipient list every time you send out an e-mail. Check the last name, not the first. What you want Paul Smith to read might infuriate Paul Jones.
4. Finally, assume that all your e-mail will be read by everybody in the Western World.

**WHEN YOU CANNOT DELIVER BAD NEWS
IN PERSON, BE VERY CAREFUL**

In fact, before you do anything, before you start typing an email or writing a letter consider these 4 rules:

1. Don't respond if you're angry. If I'm upset about something, I try NOT to respond to it for at least 24 hours. This is especially important with e-mail, where you can knock off a snotty response as quickly as you can throw a shoe.
2. If you do start writing something angry, get rid of it immediately—never send it. For example, if I simply MUST vent, I write my response as quickly as I can, get all the bad stuff out of my system—and then I delete it or throw it away.
3. Advance your objective in your response. When I really respond, I make sure that what I write advances my goal. That almost always means I stay close to the simple facts and make positive statements. This is especially important when you are in troubled waters.
4. Never say 'never'. It's better to move to an absolute position gradually. More often than not, you will discover an acceptable compromise along the way.

It is so easy to say the wrong thing when you write it down whether it's on a computer screen or on paper because there is a natural temptation to be firm and definitive. And if you are upset with something or objecting to something, it is easy to take what you consider to be a subtle shot.

IT'S ALWAYS BETTER TO DELIVER
UNPLEASANT NEWS IN PERSON.

Communicating troublesome information in writing can cause misunderstandings. It almost always takes much longer than necessary, and it can sometimes damage a relationship permanently. But the worst thing about written communication is that it is unilateral. You can say whatever you want to (you can't be interrupted), but you can't see the other person's eyes. This is a big disadvantage, especially when you're talking about something bad, uncomfortable, complicated, etc.

When you deliver difficult news in person you can read the other person's body language and make appropriate adjustments in what you're saying. When you are discussing a tricky proposal or contract, you can stop to clarify misunderstandings or to shed more light on issues of concern.

And that's not to mention the back-and-forth. Many times, I have gone into a discussion absolutely sure of my point of view—only to be won over to the other person's position in a matter of minutes. (If you are open-minded and have success as your objective, this happens quite often.) Here's the way it works: I begin to explain my position. I am interrupted, politely. The other person quickly shows me that I don't have all the information . . . or points out that I misunderstood something . . . or sometimes simply gives me a better idea. And, presto, the conversation is over! Good show! You are right. Let's do it that way.

So when you can, make an appointment to meet the other person for lunch. Or get up from your chair and take a walk across the office. Sit down and look into his or her eyes. And before you say one word, smile.

[KEY POINT]

Leaders don't let problem employees and complainers commandeer their day. They don't try to solve their employees' problems, even if they can. Instead, they give the employees the opportunity to solve their problems for themselves. And if they can't, and it's effecting their work performance, leaders let these employees go.

CHAPTER 26:
WHAT TO DO WITH PROBLEM EMPLOYEES (AND THEIR PROBLEMS)

"The important thing is this: to be able at any moment to sacrifice what we are for what we could become."
~Charles Du Bos (Approximations, 1922-37)

Every workplace seems to have one, the problem employee. The one person who is always dumping his problems on you or whining about one thing or another.

This ceaseless complainer takes your time. He steals your energy. And he diverts your attention. If you try to help, you discover that the problems seem to escalate. The more attention you pay to him, the more things he finds to complain about.

Your impulse to help him is human, but troublesome, and is based on a common but wrongheaded notion: that the employee's job is merely to show up in the morning, willing to work while his boss's job is to figure out what he should do, show him how to do it, and motivate him to do it with enthusiasm.

There is certainly something in the nature of the boss/employee relationship that involves care. The boss is in an advantaged position. He is, with respect to the relationship, more powerful, more connected and generally more knowledgeable.

This suggests a responsibility: that you use your advantages fairly. It may also suggest a sort of workplace noblesse oblige—that since you may have the power/knowledge/contacts to help him, you should do so.

WHY YOU SHOULDN'T HELP YOUR EMPLOYEES WITH THEIR PROBLEMS

The problem with noblesse oblige, however, is that it creates a relationship that is based on dependency. An employee given to asking for favors or complaining will likely get worse the more you accommodate him.

If you find that you spend a lot of your time solving employee problems and answering employee complaints examine your motives for doing so.

Are you guilty of misguided responsibility? Or are you challenged by the opportunity to show your stuff? Could your motivation be a sort of vanity?(What better way to demonstrate your skills than by fixing something someone else can't?

When you succumb to such temptations you perpetuate two mistakes simultaneously: You waste your valuable time by taking it away from a more profitable endeavor, and you reinforce the nonproductive behavior of your employee.

Employees who are allowed to shift their problems upwards are like spoiled children," says Hank Trisler, author of *No Bull Selling and No Bull Sales Management*.[55] And Larry Schulz, author of *Selling When You Hate to Sell: A Guide To Getting In Gear When You Fear Sales*, says, "A child is quick to blame someone else. It's up to the manager to point the employee in the right direction."[56]

You don't have to be rude to the complainer. But you do have to

---

55 Trisler, Hank *No Bull Selling*, Bantam ; Reissue edition (April 1, 1985), *No Bull Sales Management*, Bantam Books-Audio; (February 1987)
56 Schulz, Larry *Selling When You Hate to Sell: A Guide To Getting In Gear When You Fear Sales*, Schulz Sales and Marketing; (December 1, 1999)

let him know that his complaints will not work with you. Listen briefly, but don't indulge him.

The main thing is to give the chronic complainer the message that business is not about him and his problems. Let him know that the solutions must come from him.

SALES EMPLOYEES: A SPECIAL CASE

In the sales arena, most objections are merely camouflage for a deeper problem: The complainer is afraid of something in the sales process. He masks his fear by mentioning objections that he hears, and the objections never end. The real problem is that he hasn't the guts to close the sale, but he's afraid to say so.

"Lies are convenient because they keep (salespeople) out of action," Steve Chandler, author of *17 Lies That Are Holding You Back And The Truth That Will Set You Free*, told Selling Power magazine. "But a good sales manager can point out these falsehoods and allow someone's self-esteem to keep climbing."[57]

HOW TO STOP A CHRONIC COMPLAINER

I've run into my share of chronic complainers over the years, and I have tried all kinds of ways to respond to them. Basically, nothing works except a firm and direct reorientation. You have to let them know that your job is not to sympathize with their troubles but to demand and receive performance from them. Ask them if they can understand that. If they cannot, then you must let them go. If they can understand how they need to behave, tell them very directly that the next time they have a problem they need to do the following things before coming to you:

- Ascertain the real problem. You don't want to waste time and energy fixing situations that aren't really broken.

57 Chandler, Steve *17 Lies That Are Holding You Back And The Truth That Will Set You Free* Renaissance Books; (September 15, 2001)

- Define the problem as precisely as possible. The finer the definition, the easier it will be to discover a solution.
- Come up with at least three possible solutions.
- Decide which is the best solution and explain that decision.

You may need to make this a formal procedure. You will definitely need to enforce it. You may get a little grumbling at first, but before long your complainer will be trained to solve his own problems and you'll hear from him less and less as time goes by. If you are lucky, he will soon become adept at overcoming his own problems and may eventually turn into a top-notch employee.

EMPLOYEE PERFORMANCE PROBLEMS

Employee performance problems and the like are a different matter. If you're having a problem with an individual on your team, from poor work performance, to excessive time spent making personal phone calls, it affects everyone. Your instinct is to call a meeting and give a speech that addresses the problem. You won't mention names or point fingers. You figure the message will get through. It will, but maybe not to the person who needs it most. He'll realize that it's "about him" and either freeze up from embarrassment or freeze up from resentment.

It's much better to solve individual problems personally. Have a one-on-one meeting. Or write him a personal memo. If necessary, make two or three attempts. After the employee has used up his allotted second chances, it's time to transfer him to someone who still believes in him or fire him.

[**KEY POINT**]

Leaders understand how to maintain a top-notch working team by firing the weakest employees. But they don't simply fire people at will. They follow a firing process. This includes having more than one discussion with the employee in question and documenting every meeting and conversation.

CHAPTER 27:
HOW TO FIRE PEOPLE (WITHOUT THE AGONY)

"Almost all of our relationships begin and most of them continue as forms of mutual exploitation, a mental or physical barter, to be terminated when one or both parties run out of goods."
~W.H. Auden

The secret to having a top-notch working team is to compose it of the very best people. That's the toughest job in business because it requires you to do two very difficult things:

1. Find and hire truly excellent people
2. Correct and eventually fire weak employees

The first job is important but almost never urgent. That means it's seldom done except by people who exert extraordinary control over their time. The second job is difficult. You have to admit that you hired the wrong person, work hard to get him to improve, and then let him go just as soon as you realize he'll never improve. That process is exhausting psychologically, intellectually, and emotionally. But it's even worse if you're firing skills aren't up to par, and you're firing the wrong way.

ARE YOU FIRING THE WRONG WAY?

For example, everyone will agree that it's unpleasant to "let some-one go." That's why we often keep mediocre employees much longer than we should. When we finally make the hard decision to fire some-one, the decision that we probably should have made months or even years earlier, the impulse is to do it immediately. You want to act quickly and decisively because you're afraid that if you don't you may lose your resolve and keep him. But don't do that. Abrupt, unantici-pated terminations are unnecessary, unfair, and legally dangerous. And they often have undesirable side effects.

I've just experienced several such terminations secondhand. The employees were let go for good reasons, but only the people who did the firing knew what they were. All others concerned like fellow workers, friends, and vendors were shocked. Even the fired employees were surprised. The results were very messy and will take months and months to clean up. Truth be told, there is a right way to fire people.

> Experts suggest that more than 250,000 workers are terminated illegally each year and can seek legal action.[58]

FIRING THE RIGHT WAY

I've learned many lessons about firing. And from them, I've estab-lished 8 steps to make the firing process less agonizing:

1. Make the decision to fire as early as you can. Since great employees show their true colors almost immediately, it real-ly shouldn't take more than two weeks to a month to decide. Set high standards. Be objective. If the employee isn't what you're looking for, do it.

2. As soon as possible after you have decided, bring the employee in for a candid talk. Explain your dissatisfaction carefully. Don't make any character judgments, even if you have them. Don't

---

tell him, explicitly or otherwise, that he is dumb or lazy
or untrustworthy. Instead,
make specific complaints.
Only criticize the behavior,
not the employee.

> More than 3.8 of every 100
> employees are fired or
> resign from their jobs each
> and every month.[59]

3. Try to engage the employee
in a discussion about his own career objectives. Ask him how
the job he's doing meets his goals. You may very well discover that he is not happy with what he's doing. This may result
in a very pleasant agreement about his future, one that puts
him somewhere else, with your support and no ill will on his
part.
4. Document this first meeting in writing.
5. If it makes sense, outplace him to another department or division; but never because you want to pass along the headache to
someone else. And if he has strong skills that might work better
somewhere else, by all means give him a recommendation.
6. If you can't send him elsewhere and his performance doesn't
immediately and permanently improve, have one more formal
warning session. Again, be very specific with your complaints.
At this time, let him know that he may be terminated if the
problems continue.
7. Document this second meeting in writing.
8. When the day comes consider having someone "neutral" there
to witness the firing. Make it short and businesslike. Again, be
sure to say nothing personal. Thank him for "giving it a go"
and then stand up and walk him to the door.

How long does all of this take? This whole process outlined above
could happen in a period as short as two weeks to a month.

Yes, firing is an awful job. But it's much worse if you do it poorly.
Firing is a skill, and if you're going to be an effective leader you need
to learn how to do it right.

---

59 Small Business Guide, *BusinessWeek Online*, http://businessweek.findlaw.com/employmentbook/hfchp8.html

CHAPTER 28:

THE SECRET TO GETTING EVERY-BODY (INCLUDING THE LAGGARDS) TO BE MORE PRODUCTIVE

"Men can be stimulated by hope or driven by fear, but the hope and the fear must be vivid and immediate if they are to be effective without producing weariness."
~Bertrand Russell

Businesses are spending billions of dollars every year trying to inspire employees to work harder, smarter, and with more care. A great deal of the expense goes toward what I'd describe as "feel good" products—books, t-shirts, coffee mugs, retreats and games that seek to inspire employees to feel (and presumably think) better about their company and their jobs.

I've always been suspicious about these sorts of products. Although well intentioned, they strike me as being a bad combination of manipulation and superficiality. I put them in the same mental pigeonhole as cheerleaders and Club Med counselors—the cheery people from hell.

And it's not just products that commit this sort of crime. People do too. How about those spunky, cherub faced executives who can't seem to stop telling you how swell work is? There are other ways to motivate employees. The methods I prefer are a bit less fun but in the long run more effective.

OLD FASHIONED MOTIVATION TECHNIQUES WORK WONDERS

I'm talking about old-fashioned leadership practices that have been used to successfully motivate employees for decades. Practices like:

- Creating an inspiring vision.
- Setting high standards.
- Giving employees power
- Making them responsible
- Providing them with feedback.
- Establishing a sense of momentum

Recognizing that motivated employees tend to be more productive, business leaders should want to do everything they can to inspire motivation. But since resources like time and money are usually limited, it makes sense to emphasize the most effective motivational techniques.

In 30 years of managing employees I've tried just about every motivational trick in the book. Some of the ideas I had the greatest faith in turned out to be very ineffective. Other ideas that I originally spurned were extremely powerful. Overall, here's what I've observed:

- Mugs and tee shirts: A total waste of time. If anything they make the company that provides them (and the people that use them) look foolish.
- Pep Rallies: A stupid waste of money. Yes, they can be fun. But providing employees with a good time is not the same thing as motivating them. I'm not against business-sponsored fun so long as you don't delude yourself into thinking you are doing something you're not. Corporate pep rallies are tax-

deductible distractions.

- Inspirational posters, booklets, messages. (See my comments on mugs and tee shirts.)
- Inspirational speeches. This is a tricky one. If the person who gives the speech is respected and if his remarks are sincere and taken as sincere, then such speeches can be greatly motivating. The key is sincerity. It's not something you can fake.
- Financial Incentives: Another tricky subject. I used to be a big believer in attaching a monetary inducement to virtually any goal I set. But I found, over many years of trial and error, that they failed to work more often than they worked. I think I understand why. Money is not the primary motivating factor for most people. Furthermore, incentive-based compensation is unsettling to most workers. As a general rule I favor paying employees a good salary (a little bit more than they could get elsewhere) supplemented by a small but helpful discretionary bonus (given by his immediate supervisor).
- Creating a Vision: Essential. The vision itself needn't be crystal clear. But it does need to be attractive.
- Communicating that Vision. It's not enough to have an idea in your head. Put it in the heads (and hearts) of the people who work for you. The more effectively you can communicate your vision, the more likely it will be accomplished.
- Setting High Standards. Necessary but sometimes difficult. Don't compromise with your standards. Find a way to help your employees achieve them.
- Empowering Your People: The more power you give away, the more power you'll have. Leaders who want to control things end up with less control, less productivity and less job satisfaction. Surround yourself with good people, give them goals and standards and then get out of their way.
- Assigning Responsibility. When you give an employee the power to be in charge of something, give him also the responsibility to do it right. To the right employee, responsibility feels like a benefit. If you have someone working for you who feels differently—who wants as little responsibility as possible, for example—start looking for a replacement.

- Providing feedback. Creating a vision, establishing goals and providing power and responsibility are important requirements of effective leadership but giving your leaders regular feedback on what you like and not like is important too. Find a way to comment on employees' work and progress as often as possible.
- Establishing Momentum. One of the most important jobs of the leader is to give everyone on the team the sense that things are moving forward. Being a part of progress is always energizing. And energy, as much as anything else, is the thing that will make the difference between success and failure.

THE TRUTH ABOUT MOTIVATING YOUR EMPLOYEES

Scan the above list and you will notice a correlation between effectiveness and hard work. The easiest motivators—mugs and posters—are generally the least effective. The hard work of communicating your vision, establishing and reinforcing goals and providing specific, personal feedback will give you the best long-term results.

One of best insights I ever had on this subject came from an old book I found in a New York City used bookstore. It was called *Motivation in the Real World: The Fine Art of Getting Extra Effort from Everyone-Including Yourself* and it was authored by a Saul Gellerman, who had spent most of his career training and motivating people for corporations.[60]

Gellerman observed that in any work environment, workers tend to perform in accordance with a bell-shaped curve. A few lead the pack, a few lag behind, and most crowd into the comfortable middle.

The secret to understanding motivation, Gellerman argued, is to realize that workers don't walk around with a fixed idea of what is good poor or ordinary work. Instead, they decide how hard they should be working based upon how hard people work in the group they happen to be in at the moment.

Gellerman's theory is based on an interesting observation—that people tend to perform in relative, not absolute, terms. High perform-

---

60 Gellerman, Saul. *Motivation in the Real World: The Fine Art of Getting Extra Effort from Everyone-Including Yourself*, Plume; (September 1993)

ers, in other words, take a measure of how well and hard others are working and then find a way to do better than that. Lower performers look at the same average and say to themselves, "How can I get away with doing less than that?"

If that's true then it stands to reason that one of the most effective ways to motivate people is by establishing high standards. In theory, any time you can get one group to improve its productivity, the others will follow.

Gellerman believes in focusing your attention on the middle group. If you do that, he says, then the over- and under-performers will make the appropriate adjustments. If, for example, you are trying to improve the speed at which your customer service people answer phones and deal with problems, determine first off what the average speed is currently and then establish a new, higher "average" standard.

By getting your ordinary customer service people to meet these ordinary standards the better people will automatically raise their levels of performance above that standard just as the laggards will reduce their outputs to just below normal.

SET HIGHER STANDARDS FOR YOUR BUSINESS

The trick may be to set gradually higher standards for relatively unimportant things that nevertheless relate directly to job performance. For example, the length of time your employees have for breaks, whether they are allowed to make personal calls on company time, and so on. You could expect them to get to work at least 15 minutes early. You could require them to address one another formally. And you might want to establish a dress code, though in my experience a dress code doesn't seem to make a difference.

The point is not to be Draconian but to let people know that in your organization a high level of performance is considered normal. The achievers will welcome such a message. But for everybody else, it may take some getting used to. Gellerman says that the people in the middle of the bell curve and the laggers too, have other priorities. They may place the highest value not on success but on such "survival motives" as security, dependency, and conformity. That being said, when you raise your standards, it's important to make every effort to let the middling masses feel good about them.

Assure them they are not going to be hurt by these new standards, that their jobs are not in jeopardy, and that they will continue to be valued for the work they do. Remember, most of these people don't feel a need to perform better and never will. They are looking to you for protection and security. If you can convince them that they will get even more protection, security, and attention by performing at a slightly higher level; especially in regard to the less-critical issues, such as phone protocols, office manners, punctuality, etc., you may get their cooperation.

KEEPING YOUR TOP PEOPLE MOTIVATED

As for your top people, there is a way to further motivate them. To keep them busy on your most-important projects. Simply keep a folder for each project that includes a list of his objectives and the suggestions you've made to help him reach them. Once every so often, it could be a week or a month, have a formal, 30-minute, stand-up meeting to go over the list and update it. That kind of regular pressure even if gentle, will turn the tamest person into a lion.

---

4 STEPS THAT WILL BOOST *EVERYONE'S* PRODUCTIVITY

Here is the 4-step motivational model I've used to boost productivity of all of my employees, and it really works:

1. Invest in your top performers. Spend time, money, and educational resources to locate, hire, train and supply superstar employees. Don't leave this to chance.
2. Don't manage people. Manage objectives. If you want better productivity and a more motivated work force, don't spend any time worrying about how your employees feel. Focus your time and energy on the tasks ahead of you and make sure your employees are doing the same.

3. Treat people well. By this I mean do what you think is best for them. And for some people in some situations that means being tough. So forget about all the crap you read that advises all the soft stuff. Do what you have to do to make your best people work harder than they've ever worked for anyone else. Try to never do anything that will make them quit and go elsewhere.

4. Trim the branches. Fire your weakest employees and replace them with great ones. This should be a never-ending process. In every group, people arrange themselves according to personal comfort levels. The achievers move immediately to the front of the line, the mediocre people find the middle, and the snails find the tail. The way to get your group to perform at a higher level is to regularly replace your weakest links with new, stronger ones. The perfect situation would be to regularly lose your worst employee and replace him with a genuine superstar. *(For more information on how to fire people, turn to Chapter 27.)*

SUMMARY

Throughout this book, we've looked at the qualities it takes to succeed in leadership today. Qualities I've witnessed among many great leaders during my 30 years in business.

My goal in writing *Power and Persuasion* was to help you become a more effective leader by planting a few seeds that would later on have a lasting impact on your career. Since I've seen these ideas work so well in my life, I can't help but believe they'll help you. In fact, I'm quite certain that if you adopt even a few of these qualities as your own, you cannot help but improve your leadership skills.

A number of the ideas and experiences I've shared in these pages run contrary to mainstream theory, and some may be unfamiliar to you. As you've read through them and considered them, I hope you've come to recognize the value of being a *persuasive* leader. Not a power broker, not a consensus taker, not a team builder, not a micromanager or a hand-holder...but a leader who *inspires* others to follow your vision.

Let's take a moment to quickly revisit some of those "contrarian" ideas:

- **Effective leaders do NOT "look out for Number One."** The great leaders I know don't spend much time thinking about themselves. Instead they focus on goals—on growing the business, on improving the product, on pleasing the customer. Effective leaders are outwardly focused, which means they tend to be people-friendly, loyal, and eager to improve things. They're not concerned about where they fall in the pecking order—whether in the industry or in the business. They're internally driven. They focus on work, not politics…on goals, not crisis. And they purposefully use their strongest talents. Creative leadership is one of the most important skills you can learn.

- **Effective leaders understand how to follow.** Remember the story I told in Chapter One about learning to ballroom dance? You can lead by throwing your weight around and pushing or yanking your followers around with you, as I was doing in those first few lessons. Or you can learn the secrets of leadership and arrive at your destination sooner, with better results, and much happier followers. But that means putting yourself in their shoes to see things from their perspective.

- **Effective leaders know when NOT to be competitive.** Competition has its place in business, but it is not nearly as important as cooperation and sharing. I've achieved most of my success by forcing myself to ignore my naturally competitive instincts and focus on the business. Rather than worry about how a colleague or competitor might be gaining on me (or surpassing me), I do better when I think about improving the product or doing a better job selling it. When businesses environments get too competitive, lots of bad things happen. An overly competitive environment can lead to unproductive behaviors, such as colleagues withholding important information from one another, taking pot shots at each other, and spending a lot of time beating people down instead of improving products and sales. But cooperating, helping, innovating, and sharing, can lead to a long, happy career. Remember, the good things you do in business—the help you give others, the information that you share, etc.—will show you to be someone other people want to be around. Having that reputation is an asset that will repay you in countless ways, be they financial or personal.

- **Effective leaders are considerate.** The best leaders I know focus on making things better, not on being liked. But they achieve corporate goals by treating everyone around them with kindness and consideration. Arrogance and rudeness, they realize, are counterproductive. If your employees actively dislike you, they'll have a hard time following your lead. If you want to reach all of your business goals in the shortest amount of time, you have to learn to be instinctively considerate.

- **Effective leaders attach deadlines to their goals.** This is not a "contrarian" idea, but it's so important that it has to be included in this summary chapter. Great leaders are not just good at setting goals and communicating them, they know how to delegate them to responsible people and attach deadlines to them. Getting to success requires a plan—one that is well thought out, written down, and developed into specific objectives. Furthermore, those objectives must be communicated clearly, and have standards of quality and deadlines attached to them.

- **Effective leaders take follow-up to the next level.** Serious follow-up involves much more than sending a series of urgent reminders. It requires the willingness to set aside time to make sure the objective is clearly understood, to discuss and review the plan for accomplishing it, and to help brainstorm solutions to any problems. This is truly a secret to great leadership—and though it's relatively simple, it's rarely followed.

- **Effective leaders create a culture of accountability.** If you expect your business to grow, you have to develop a sense of accountability among your staff, so they feel a sense of responsibility for the success of projects specifically and the well being of the business overall. To develop accountability, you have to trust people to carry out their responsibilities. If you micromanage people because you don't trust them, not only will they *not* feel accountable, they will become resentful.

- **Effective leaders don't try to control everything.** If you want to be a strong leader, you must learn to give up control over certain tasks. Delegation is essential to leadership because it frees up time for the things you should be focusing on—like improving your business.

- **Effective leaders listen as well as talk.** This is another conventional but important idea. You don't have to be the world's most sympathetic listener to be a great leader, but you must listen. Effective leaders listen first. After they're done listening, they listen some more. When they do speak, they measure their words, realizing that saying more often means saying less. And they pay attention to the other person's concerns and interests.

- **Effective leaders understand** *proper* **teamwork.** Don't buy into the notion that teamwork means giving every person, every idea, every suggestion, and every interest equal support. Successful business leaders treat all of their team members with equal respect, but have different expectations for each one. Those expectations are based on individual performance, not idealistic beliefs.

- **Effective leaders don't become therapists for their employees.** If you spend a lot of your time solving problems and answering employee complaints, you need to examine your motives for doing so. Succumbing to this temptation steals valuable time from more profitable endeavors, and reinforces the nonproductive behavior of the employee. Don't indulge such behavior. While you might listen briefly, make it clear that the solution lies with him, not you.

- **Effective leaders don't manipulate better performances out of people.** Rather than resorting to feel-good incentives, such as books, T-shirts, retreats, etc. to manipulate your employees into working harder and smarter, motivate them by spurring their own inner desire to do better. Create an inspiring vision, set high standards, give employees power, make them accountable, offer feedback, establish a sense of momentum. These methods may not be as "fun" as a rah-rah retreat, but they are infinitely more effective.

Vision is the first attribute of leadership. Unless you have an idea about how your business/product/service can be better, you can't lead your employees at all. You can only confuse them.

Once you have a mental picture of your goal, your next step is to project that picture so that everyone on your team – including your employees, colleagues, vendors, and other supporters – can see it.

So if vision is the first attribute of great leadership, communication is the second. Being able to show your vision, however nebulous it is, is a skill that can be learned. The secret to doing that is relatively simple. Identify the critical ideas and express them, both in writing and orally, as clearly as you can.

But having a vision and communicating it are not enough. Not only does your support team need to see your goal, they must embrace it. Here is where persuasion comes into play. If you can develop the skill to convince others that your ideas are worth following, you will have the power to make truly astonishing changes.

Great change requires power. And lasting, market- and culture-changing power comes from persuasion. First vision. Then communication. Then persuasion. And, finally, power.

Great leaders inspire great work. They do so by finding and nurturing extraordinary talent, setting substantial goals, making those goals seem exciting, and then keeping the entire team focused on all the necessary tasks required to achieve them. Great leaders are willing to do the hard thinking, make the tough decisions, and get the job done. They have the vision, knowledge, skills, and good ideas. But more importantly, they've learned how to get people to embrace those ideas and work to achieve them, even in the face of adversity and criticism.

Inspiring that kind of work isn't an easy thing to do. It takes a rare combination of openness and resolution, toughness and compassion, cooperation and competition.

The good news is that leadership, like so many other important skills (communication, negotiation, analytical thinking, etc.), can be learned. I hope that within these pages you've discovered ideas—maybe new ones, maybe forgotten ones—that have helped to renew your own vision and inspire you to become the great leader you want to be.

RECOMMENDED READINGS

Adams, Douglas, *The Hitchhiker's Guide to the Galaxy*, Ballantine Books: September 27, 1995.

Altier, William J. *The Thinking Man's Toolbox: Effective Processes for Problem Solving and Decision Making*, New York: Oxford University Press, 1999.

Anderson, Dave, *No-Nonsense Leadership: Real World Strategies To Maximize Personal & Corporate Potential*, Creative Broadcast Concepts: November 2001.

Boothman, Nicholas *How to Make People Like You In 90 Seconds Or Less*, Workman Publishing Company; (September 18, 2000)

Buzan, Barry, Buzan, Tony, *Mind Map Book: How To Use Radiant Thinking to Maximize Your Brain's Untapped Potential*, Plume: March 1996

Chandler, Steve *17 Lies That Are Holding You Back And The Truth That Will Set You Free* Renaissance Books; (September 15, 2001)

Charan, Ram *What the CEO Wants You to Know: How Your Company Really Works*, Crown Business; 1st edition (February 13, 2001)

Covey, Steven R. *7 Habits of Highly Effective People*, Simon & Schuster; 1st edition: September 15, 1990.

Diener, Marc, *Deal Power: 6 Foolproof Steps To Making Deals of Any Size*, Henry Holt & Company, Inc.; January 1998.

Emerson, Ralph Waldo, *The Conduct of Life*, University Press of the Pacific; April 2002.

Fisher , Roger, Ury, Bill, Patton, Bruce. *Getting To Yes: Negotiating Agreement Without Giving In*, Penguin USA; 2nd edition: December 1991.

Fisher, Marsh *The Ideafisher: How to Land That Big Idea-And Other Secrets of Creativity in Business*, Petersons Guides, 2000.

Fox, Jeffrey J. *How to Become CEO: The Rules for Rising to the Top of Any Organization*, Hyperion Press, October 1998.

Gelb, Michael J. *Thinking For A Change: Discovering The Power To Create, Communicate, and Lead*, Crown Publishers: New York: 1995.

Gellerman, Saul, *Motivation In The Real World*, Random House, 1995.

Gellerman, Saul. *Motivation in the Real World: The Fine Art of Getting Extra Effort from Everyone-Including Yourself*, Plume; (September 1993).

Gladwell, Malcolm *The Tipping Point: How Little Things Can Make A Big Difference* Back Bay Books; (January 7, 2002).

Greene, Robert, *48 Laws of Power*, Penguin: September 2000.

Heller, Robert, Hindle, Tim *How To Delegate*, DK Publishing, January 1997.

Hoff, Ron, *I Can See You Naked*, Andrews McMeel Publishing: October 1992.

Hoffer, Eric *The Passionate State of Mind*, 1954, Buccaneer Books: Reprint, August 1998.

L 'Amour, Louis, *Education of a Wandering Man*, Bantam Books: Reissue 1989.

LeBon, Paul, Karam, Sara, *Escape From Voicemail Hell / Boost Your Productivity By Making Voicemail Work For You*, ParLeau Publishing, October, 1999.

Lindbergh, Charles A. *Autobiography of Values*, 1978, Harvest Books: Reprint 1992.

Lyles, Dick *Winning Ways: 4 Secrets For Getting Results By Working Well With People* Berkley Pub Group; 1st edition (December 4, 2001).

Russo, J. Edward, Shoemaker, Paul J.H., *Decision Traps*, Doubleday: 1989.

Safir, Leonard, Safire, William, *Leadership: A Treasury of Great Quotations for Those Who Aspire to Lead* (Galahad Books, September 2000).

Santayana, George *The Life of Reason: Reason in Society*, 1905, Dover Publications: Reissue: 1983.

Schulz, Larry *Selling When You Hate to Sell: A Guide To Getting In Gear When You Fear Sales*, Schulz Sales and Marketing; (December 1, 1999).

Shell, Richard G. *Bargaining For Advantage: Negotiating Strategies For Reasonable People*, Penguin USA Reissue edition: June 5, 2000.

The Instant Consultant, Executive Excellence Publishing, June 2002.

The Leader of the Future, The Drucker Foundation, New York: 1996.

Trisler, Hank *No Bull Selling*, Bantam; Reissue edition (April 1, 1985), *No Bull Sales Management*, Bantam Books–Audio; (February 1987).

INDEX

SPECIAL: For Readers of *Power and Persuasion*

Become Wealthier, Healthier, And Wiser With Practical Money-Making And Life Secrets From A Multimillionaire

The purpose of Michael Masterson's daily online e-newsletter, Early to Rise (ETR) is quite simple: to get it's readers to succeed in life. In this daily email advisory service, Michael, a semi-retired multimillionaire, shares proven, easy-to-follow approaches for becoming wealthier, healthier, and wiser; and arms you with valuable insights and practical tools that help you dramatically improve your life.

When you read ETR each morning, you will be reminded of what is possible for you:

For Your Wealth: ETR can show you how to get control of your finances, develop financially valuable skills, and begin building, or adding to, your wealth. It can show you how to turn your life around in 24 hours and steadily get richer — by increasing the income you already have ... by adding a second, active source of income... by investing profitably in real estate and other financial markets.... and by living like a billionaire without spending like one.

For Your Health: You don't need to spend hours every day training and keeping to a strict diet to become healthy, fit, agile, and pain-free. You can have great health by following the ETR-designed health-and-fitness program for busy professionals. Build muscle by lifting weights just twice a week. Increase your cardiovascular fitness threefold. Eat like a king — including pretty much all the meat, fish, nuts, and berries you want (cheese too!) — without putting on a pound.

For Your Wisdom: ETR will help you achieve your personal-growth goals by advising you on how to become a better speaker, writer, thinker, and listener. You'll build your vocabulary; increase your knowledge of good living (art, wine, etc.); and learn how to impress your boss, satisfy your most discerning customers, charm new acquaintances, develop loyalty among your employees and friends, and come to more tranquility and simplicity in your life.

Practically every day, someone writes ETR to explain how some suggestion changed their life ... how income grew, job satisfaction increased, health improved, productivity doubled, profits boomed, stress was reduced, etc.

If you like the thought of being good at everything you do and enjoying all of life's experiences... ETR will give you the kick-start you need to reach your dreams. A better, brighter, fuller, and happier future is at your fingertips. Just go for it!

Now as a reader of *Power and Persuasion,* you can immediately sign up for a **free trial subscription** to the *Early to Rise* daily advisory:

www.earlytorise.com/SuccessPartnership.htm